CIRCUS SMIRKUS ®

Circus Smirkus: 25 Years of Running Home to the Circus
By Rob Mermin and Rob Gurwitt

The stories in this book depict actual people and events. No names have been changed, in order to protect the right of all involved to proclaim truthfully, "Yes, I really did run home to the circus!"

Published by The Circus Barn Inc., 1 Circus Road, Greensboro, VT
www.smirkus.org

Design by Serena Fox Design Company
Cover Photo by Harry Powers
Smirkus Logo by Diana Cunningham and Rob Mermin

Library of Congress Control Number 2012937424
ISBN 978-0-9854021-0-5

Printed in the U.S. by Villanti in Milton, Vermont

First Edition: June 2012
10 9 8 7 6 5 4 3 2 1

It is with circus-going
as it is with Sin.
One sin is always followed by a long procession of others.
He who goes to the Circus is Lost Forever.

—Burlington [VT] Free Press & Times, July 27, 1883

PREFACE

By Rob Gurwitt

There is a moment in each swing of a trapeze when anything can happen.
It comes at the very peak, when the performer has stopped rising
but has yet to start back down. For that instant she is weightless. She can flip off the bar and grab it with her hands, dive backward and drop until her feet catch her or let go and simply hang, for the blink of an eye, suspended in midair.
It's the moment when you, in the audience, forget to breathe.

The artist has to pay for that moment. The laws of physics demand it, and they exact their toll at the bottom of the swing, where the g-forces are strongest and a performer is in greatest peril of falling. This is part of a trapeze act, too, an exercise in strength and resolve that usually passes unnoticed by the watching crowd. Unless, of course, the artist misjudges and falls.

You could think of a circus in the same fashion. For a couple of light-filled hours anything can happen. People fly through the air; they send impossible numbers of juggling clubs cascading about them; they walk, dance, even leap and flip on the merest filaments of wire; they fling their bodies at exhilarating velocity across space, talk to animals, create heart-melting beauty and, in the next breath, gleeful pandemonium. They so command our attention that for a brief period the tent, the ring at its center and all the people inside are ageless, suspended in time.

Yet the laws of nature can't be denied. If we could peer into a circus before its opening performance, take it all in at once, we would see that. We would see that its time-stopping magic is paid for with muscles hardened by training, with aches and bruises, with the unseeing stare of utter concentration and the dry tinder of human ambition. We would see that underneath the daily triumphs there can also be moments of great peril for the entire circus, overcome only by dint of endless work and determination. We would see that circuses trace an arc, too, and that if you want to know their story you have to watch the whole swing, not just those incandescent moments at the top.

We're on a hill in the Northeast Kingdom of Vermont. It's July and the grass is lush and green, a gift of heavy rains in the spring and early summer. In the distance stretch the unchanging mountains and woods, and below us the fields of a ramshackle farmstead. At our feet is a large circus tent, its pennants slack in the still air. It is midmorning, a brilliantly sunny day, and the white, blue and yellow tent almost blazes in the light. In a few hours, the field will fill with cars as hundreds of people converge for the first public performance of a new Circus Smirkus show.

For a quarter of a century, Smirkus has been a part of summer life not just for the crowds around its home in Greensboro, Vermont, but throughout New England. It is not your usual small traveling circus. Its performers are kids and teenagers, ages 10 to 18, and from around the time school lets out for the summer until it's almost time to go back, they inhabit a world with a few extra, especially vivid, colors.

Before we get into that, though, we should set one thing straight. Even from our perch on the hill, we can see that what lies below us is not what you'd think of when you hear the words "youth circus." There is nothing cute or precious or make-believe about it. The main tent, designed and built in Italy, is big enough to fit a crowd of 800 people and a mass of industrial-strength rigging. Behind it is a changing and props tent, in front a couple of concessions tents crowded with paraphernalia, cotton candy and popcorn machines and large coolers of water. When Smirkus heads out on the road, it takes along a couple dozen trucks, buses and campers, a full rolling kitchen and close to 75 people. It is in every way a circus; its performers just happen to be younger than usual.

What takes place inside the tent is remarkable. Compared to the technical abilities of the performers you'd see at Ringling Bros. or the Big Apple Circus or Cirque du Soleil, Smirkus's young troupe members sometimes come up a few twists, clubs or aerial flips short. Yet none of that matters in a show, because for a few hours they immerse the audience in a glowing bath of energy, pluck and joy that is impossible to resist. First-timers to a Smirkus show come out not quite believing what they just saw and already wondering when they can go again. Fans while away the passage from youth to middle age and middle age to retirement without missing a year, simply because summer is inconceivable without it.

Yet what's happened outside the tent over the last quarter-century is just as amazing. Smirkus began as one clown's pipe dream, a funky, off-kilter, shoestring operation aimed at giving kids in a remote corner of New England the chance to get a taste of circus life. It has blossomed into the premier traveling youth circus in America, along the way establishing a wildly popular summer camp that trains hundreds of kids each year and touching thousands more through its school residencies.

Smirkus has brought performers and coaches to small-town New England from 28 countries, including Russia, Latvia, Mongolia, Colombia, England, New Zealand, Australia and Morocco, as well as from every corner of the United States, including inner-city Chicago and Indian reservations out West. It has sent its alumni off into the world, prepared for anything that Hollywood, academia, corporate and community life, and professional circuses big and small can dish out. Big-time directors and talent scouts from Ringling, Cirque du Soleil and European circuses routinely come to watch Smirkus shows and take the measure of future stars. Kids from all over the country—and, indeed, all over the world—hanker after one of its hard-earned slots. It's won international circus awards, garnered a Vermont Citation of Excellence and been featured in a film documentary, a Disney Channel series and articles too numerous to count.

Like traveling shows under canvas for 200 years, Smirkus has overcome floods, mud, power outages, illness, surly safety inspectors, vehicle breakdowns, desperately late arrivals and one terrible traffic accident to put on every show on its schedule for 25 years. It has skirted bankruptcy numerous times, fended off corporate takeover attempts and been infiltrated by the Soviet KGB and Chinese officialdom. It has seen "fine friendships, high adventures, low comedy, real tragedy, true loves, desperate dramas, immeasurable laughter and countless good times," as founder Rob Mermin says. Even after 25 years, there is nothing else like it in America.

Smirkus began as a dream, nourishes dreamers and still has its own dreams. This book is one of them—a chance to look back, take stock and tell some good stories. It is a chance to see the entire arc of Smirkus's swing.

Watching from the top of our hill, we can tell the show's about to begin. The field at our feet is crammed with cars. From the tent comes the clamor of hundreds of voices. The last stragglers rush toward the entrance, just as a cymbal-clash and jaunty swell of horns announce the first rush of tumblers bursting through the curtain and a voice booms from the ring, "Sit back, relax and enjooooo-ooooyyyyy the show!"

PROLOGUE

By Circus Smirkus Founder Rob Mermin

I never daydreamed of running off to join the circus. No small traveling show ever came to my town. No Big Top set up in our fields to proclaim a world of exotic animals and equally fascinating human beings.

As a child in the '50s, I was an explorer in the backyard woods of my New England hometown, a wanderer in the broad world of my vagabond imagination.

My first glimpse of the foreign world of circus showfolk was at a state fair, looking through a fence at a bare-chested, muscled man practicing behind a caravan. He was balancing on a low wire, waving his arms in the sun. A beautiful dark-eyed woman next to him was hanging wet spangled tights on an improvised clothesline. The man suddenly glanced over at me, perfectly at rest on the wire, arms up, one leg calmly waving in the air. The woman looked up and smiled at me. I moved on, holding my father's hand. What extraordinary race of people were they?

Fifteen years later I was hanging wet baggy clown trousers on an improvised clothesline behind my caravan at a state fair and I glanced over at a kid watching from behind a fence. Our eyes met and held.

Who are you? his wide eyes said.

I was you once, mine silently replied. *What is your dream going to be?*

He moved on, holding his father's hand, glancing back.

I didn't run off to join the circus until I was in college, in the late '60s. I was draft age in Chicago during the political traumas of 1968. I was tear-gassed minding my own business on the streets of Paris in 1969. I disliked the fervency of crowds. My radicalism was quieter. As friends marched in civil protests and inflamed political debate hung in the air like an angry cloud, I wondered how I could best contribute to the kind of world we envisioned. What would a society feel like in which there was humor without malice, laughter without scorn, common sense in public discourse, decency in human relations, delight in sharing skills without aggressive competition?

When I was 19 I got it into my head that circus was a physical symbol for the community I envisioned and a vehicle for everything I loved doing in the arts. I'd studied mime, acrobatics, theater, silent-film slapstick. Circus incorporated all these forms of artistry, along with an intriguing lifestyle. Circus in America, however, was dying out; the big shows had abandoned canvas tents and gone indoors to coliseums. Ringling Bros. and Barnum & Bailey clowns were aging. As Ringling opened Clown College to train a new generation of funsters, I headed to Europe. I felt a yearning for the old-time traveling tent show that played small rural towns, a past that had eluded my own childhood.

I was old enough to know I needed experience and young enough to be full of idealism. I knew that the traditional European circus world was still vibrant and clowns were respected as artists. So what else could I do but pack my bag and head out for adventure? I went looking for a circus with the goal of learning the trade and someday creating a small rural traveling circus of my own. I took the talents I possessed and the skills I had taught myself and sallied forth to find an unconventional lifestyle of renewable adventure.

The appeal of intrepid vagabonding! A daydream with determination! Circus was a mythical global subculture inhabited by an itinerant race with sawdust in their veins, a culture with its own history, lingo and traditions. I set out on a mission in search of an apprenticeship under canvas. When you take the path of adventure, you're looking for trouble—and sure to find it. At the very least I was hoping to gather stories I could tell in old age. I got everything I bargained for, and more, starting on day one...

CHAPTER ONE

MUD, MAGIC & MULES

A Clown Apprentice Discovers Mirth, Mayhem & Mischief

It's 1969.

We're in a valley somewhere in Wales.

Before us stands a circus tent belonging to Circus Hoffman. "The Wildest Show On Earth," they call themselves, and they're not exaggerating. The tent went up the night before, roustabouts setting up long bleacher seats, pounding in heavy iron stakes with 20-pound sledges, knotting thick ropes with half-hitch twists to keep the tent standing, the whole scene punctuated by a clamor of yells and curses in several languages. Now, trucks and caravans sit in a protective circle around the tent. It smells of hay, sawdust, dung and the clotted, mingled aromas of horses, camels, elephants, bears, dogs, llamas and geese.

Inside, the newest member of the circus is about to go on. His name is Rob Mermin, but his American accent already has everyone calling him "Tex." He showed up out of the blue first thing in the morning, declared himself to be a clown—not so much an out-and-out lie as a moment's wishful thinking—and was summarily packed off to a corner of the lot to smash dead cows' heads with a sledgehammer. Snacks for the lion, he was told.

Now he's about to get his first taste of life in the ring. Here's how the act is supposed to go. It's a simple animal walk-around, a chance to show off the Hoffman menagerie as the ring crew changes the set. Charlie—Karl Brenner, a bear of a German clown—is dressed as an Indian fakir, wearing a tall turban and carrying a large wicker basket and musical pipe. Sitting cross-legged in the middle of the ring, he'll play his pipe, which is attached to a hose hidden in the basket, out of which a long balloon snake will rise to dance in the air. Meanwhile, Little John, a dwarf, will enter leading a llama; Rob will follow him with a donkey. When Charlie blows the horn so hard the balloon snake pops, Little John and Rob will trot quickly around the ring and then exit to make room for the next act.

Waiting to go on, Rob notices one of the Hoffman brothers, who sees him and orders

Inside, the newest member of the circus is about to go on. His name is Rob Mermin.

him to run off and get the camel. The camel, he announces, *always* goes in this act. Rob stands there dumbly, his hopes for an easy time in the ring evaporating.

"C'mon, Tex," Hoffman grunts. "Get that bloody camel over here!"

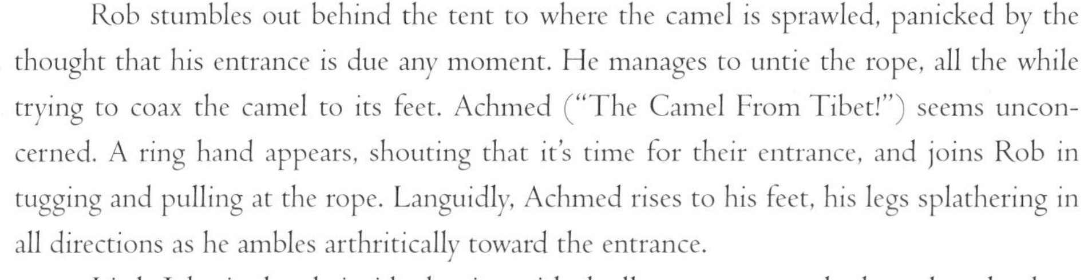

Rob stumbles out behind the tent to where the camel is sprawled, panicked by the thought that his entrance is due any moment. He manages to untie the rope, all the while trying to coax the camel to its feet. Achmed ("The Camel From Tibet!") seems unconcerned. A ring hand appears, shouting that it's time for their entrance, and joins Rob in tugging and pulling at the rope. Languidly, Achmed rises to his feet, his legs splathering in all directions as he ambles arthritically toward the entrance.

Little John is already inside the ring with the llama; someone else has taken the donkey. Rob looks around frantically for someone who can lead in the camel, when he hears, "Up ya gaw, Tex! *Ride 'em, cowboy!!!*" and feels himself hoisted by elbows and knees and tossed like a sack of flour onto the camel's back. With a sharp Hoffman slap on its rump, the camel heads for the spotlight, Rob's legs flapping in the air at each step.

Hanging on for dear life, losing his grip at each bounce and sliding down the hump toward the tail, Rob repeatedly scrambles and claws his way back up—to the boisterous delight of the crowd. Achmed lopes along, contentedly drooling and following the other animals. After what seems like an hour, Charlie's snake balloon finally bursts and the music goes double time, the signal for the animals to race around the ring and exit. *Trampled to death by a camel in Wales,* Rob thinks. Suddenly he hears Charlie's voice above the noise, yelling for him to grab the trapeze bar.

"Tex! Next time around, reach up and grab to *der shving bar!*"

Rob notices the trapeze just as he's passing underneath. Hanging onto the hump and timing it the second time around, he waits for Achmed to bounce him upward, lets go of the camel's hair, reaches for the bar and suddenly finds himself kicking wildly over an empty ring in midair. The crowd roars its approval. Rob, basking in the moment, plays up the kicks. Until the music begins for the next act, the curtain opens… and in run the elephants.

But let's leave him there for a minute, hanging in midair: a 19-year-old circus greenhorn watching a brace of very large animals barrel toward the spot where, when he lets go, he'll be sprawled. Because at this point you've got to be wondering: What on earth was he thinking?

There were some 52 circuses in Great Britain in the 1960s, and fate dealt me a forced hand from a marked deck when I stumbled into the notorious world of the Hoffman Brothers' "Wildest Show On Earth" in the mountains of northern Wales. I had been hitchhiking around looking for circus adventures I could talk about 40 years

Robin, Pete and Antonio
in Copenhagen, 1973

hence, so one evening, when I saw a circus tent sleeping in the valley below, I didn't hesitate. Itchy with adventure, I snuck under the tent and slept under the bleachers with a pillow of sawdust and straw.

I had stumbled into a real "mud show," a circus term for a company that traveled by truck and caravan and set up in muddy lots when it rained. I recall Hoffman's as the epitome of mud shows the way they must have been in America in the 1800s. Four decades later, when I mentioned to circus folks in Britain that my first show was with the Hoffmans, their mouths fell open in bemused awe that I had been with "the boys" in their heyday—and lived to tell the tale.

The five hooligan Hoffmans were rogues, rebels, ruffians, pitiless procrastinators of tasteless style. They spat with contempt upon normal laws of bureaucracy; they sneered with disdain at requests by government authority to abide by regular business practices; they ignored any attempts at discussion each week when it came to payday; they changed their phone numbers periodically; and as a matter of course they dispatched local police forces with impunity. And they did it all with a grin.

My first morning with the Hoffmans, two uniformed members of the local Welsh constabulary approached me. "Who's in charge 'ere?" one asked. I pointed to a shirtless sweaty Hoffman carrying on his shoulders a heavy stack of 16-foot wood bleacher boards. As the police approached, Hoffman dropped the boards inches away from their feet. They jumped back in alarm. Hoffman grinned and with exaggerated flourish invited the constables into his caravan. The other four brothers nonchalantly came around the corner and slipped into the caravan after them. Two minutes passed. I glanced over to see the caravan rocking. The door was flung open: here came one uniformed fellow flying through the air, landing face down in the dust, followed by the second airborne constable! The pile of uniforms scrambled to its feet and fled into the distance, growing smaller and smaller like Keystone Kops, never to be seen again. Something about permits, I found out later.

The five hooligan Hoffmans were rogues, rebels, ruffians, pitiless procrastinators of tasteless style.

Now that you know who Rob's taken up with, let's get back to him, dangling from the trapeze. It turns out that not even an approaching gang of pachyderms can quash a good showman. Rob lets go of the bar, drops into the ring, rolls into a somersault, jumps up and kicks his heels to show the audience it was all part of the act, then careens over the ring curb just in time to miss being trampled.

That's the matinee show.

At the evening show, when it comes time for the animal walk-around, one of the Hoffmans walks up, looks Rob in the eye, and says as if to no one in particular, "Ayup, someone's got ta gaw git that camel." And so begins Rob's apprenticeship in the circus.

But one other thing happens that night, too, that's worth recording. It's a jump night, and hours of work lie ahead to clear the site and move on to the next town. So after the show the animals are loaded into travel wagons; concessions get packed away; roustabouts stack bleacher boards as each section of spectators climbs down and hits the grass; and then, eventually, the tent comes down. In the end, all that's left is a circle of caravans around a circle of sawdust.

After the commotion of load-out—the hammering of sledgehammers to loosen iron stakes, the shouts and curses of the tent crew, grunts from the elephants pulling wagons out of mud, joking from the artistes who had discarded their spangles and were helping out wearing dirty coveralls and thick working gloves, the children, the bosses, everyone becoming roustabouts after a long day—suddenly it was silence. In the middle of the night, when all was finally packed up, everyone disappeared into their caravans for a bite to eat, the French over here, the Germans over there, bosses on the far end, roustabouts in the back trailers. Then seemingly on cue, with a circus sixth sense of timing, everyone came out carrying piping-hot tea, not in dainty teacups but in large, steaming bowls that you cupped in two hands. With calloused palms, you didn't get burned; the heat of the bowls transferred through the hands and was absorbed into the body, spreading out to fatigued muscles. I was bruised, battered, on the fringe of exhaustion beyond fatigue. The cute French teenage juggler smiled coyly at me. Her older brothers saw this and scowled. I knew there would be enough stories to last a lifetime—if I managed to survive. This was not your typical circus. I knew I could learn something from the Hoffman style of self-inflicted pandemonium and anarchy.

This moment—of companionship, belonging and intimacy, of satisfaction in hard work and the pleasure of having shared the rigors of entertaining an audience—will get repeated after every nighttime Hoffman show. Years later, sitting on the porch of the old Vermont farmhouse that will eventually become Smirkus headquarters, Rob will decide he has to recreate it as he revives the idea of a small country circus traveling to rural New England towns.

But he's not done with his circus apprenticeship—not by a long shot. After some time with the Hoffmans, he heads to France to study mime with Marcel Marceau and his teacher, Étienne Decroux. Mime is his first love, but in 1973, after completing college, he realizes that he cannot shake the sawdust from his veins. Pantomime may be filled with metaphor and poetry, but Rob finds himself longing for the mud and mayhem of the circus. And so he heads back to Europe with $50 and a red clown nose in his pocket....

The second time I ran off to join the circus, I gave myself three days to find one before the money ran out. After misadventures with a big show in Belgium (vulgar clowns, not to my taste) and playing the trumpet with a gypsy family performing in town squares in Lichtenstein (another dark-haired, brown-eyed daughter with scowling brothers, and a fast escape), I found myself passing through Copenhagen. Just opposite the famous Tivoli in the center of the city, I stood facing a glorious centuries-old circus building. It was Cirkus Benneweis. I bought a ticket with my last coins and got a seat upstairs. Two thousand plush velvet seats faced a ring with a 16-piece orchestra on a balcony over the ring entrance. The best acts from around the world entered through that velvety curtain. Diana Benneweis, circus princess, worked 16 white horses in a lavish Parisian gown. This show was pure class, like witnessing the golden age of 19th-century circus.

After the show I stayed watching the ring boys clean up, my thoughts zooming ahead in time. I finally had a real goal in life: I would someday join this show! This was something to work hard for, a clear objective! I figured it would take two decades of hard work, experience in smaller shows, then bigger shows, and finally—mature, experienced, ready for renown—I would return to Denmark and triumphantly perform with this show. It would take 20 years for sure, but I could make it...

Suddenly I was knocked out of my reverie by a ring boy asking if I needed help. "No, no, I just loved the show, I'm a clown myself, and..."

Before I knew it I was dragged, protesting, to the director's office, shoved in the door and offered a trial period in the show itself. You do mime? Can you fill in? One of the two clowns was ill. SNAP! So much for those 20 years.

The next morning I found myself in clown costume leading the whole circus, horses and elephants included, in the annual parade through the city, waving to the cheering crowds, shaking hands with thousands of children. The Danish royal family followed me in a golden carriage led by 16 proud prancing horses with plumes on their noble heads. What kind of fairytale was this?

I stayed three years in Copenhagen as the house clown in its famous cirkusbygningen*, or "circus building," by the Tivoli. There were misadventures aplenty. Once my clown partners—Peter Harrison, an acrobat from England, and Antonio, a wire-walking Spanish dwarf—and I were in the middle of a bank robber gag when the whole circus building erupted in chaos. I had just pulled out a fake rubber gun to*

pretend to shoot Antonio—a rubber bullet moved in slow motion on a string and bounced off his chest—when a section of the audience rose to its feet and ran crashing right into the ring. I looked up at ten men coming at me in black suits with necks thick as bulls. What in the world? One of them karate-chopped my hand holding the rubber gun, two others wrestled me to the ground, one pulled my arms behind my back. Antonio, bless his heart, only as tall as the man's waist, kicked him in the shins. Bulgarian acrobats ran in and joined in the fray. A brawl in the ring! The audience was stunned: was this part of the act? The show stopped for 20 minutes. Backstage I was frisked, shaken and interrogated. It turned out the recently exiled Greek royal family was in the audience and the bodyguards reacted instinctively when they saw a gun.

Just another day at the office.

At the Benneweis circus palace in Copenhagen, Rob learns the elements of artistic excellence at the highest levels. He sees firsthand the finesse, flair, elegance and attention to detail that spring from circus tradition and make up classic circus style. The top artists, he notices, are also the most humble and down-to-earth, confident in their accomplishments, proud of their abilities, comfortable with their skills—but feeling no need to exercise their ego. They are willing to share their skills and always ready with extraordinary stories of life on the road. Rob drinks all of it in.

It was the day after the circus season closed in Copenhagen. Three years with first-class artistes from around the world passing through the Benneweis circus building. I didn't know what to do next. My apprenticeship with famous European clowns was over—Charlie Rivel, The Francescos, Joe Jackson, Jr., the great Russian clown Popov, Karl Kossmayer...Kossmayer! I got on my bike and rode furiously through the streets of Copenhagen to get to the circus building.

Circus folks are known for not saying good-bye at the end of a long season. There are no drawn-out departures. It is a simple "See you down the road" and a wave of the hand. I got to the building just in time to see Kossmayer loading the mules in his truck, about to head down to the Netherlands, his home base for the winter with his Dutch wife, Sjoukje Dijkstra, the former world-champion and Olympic gold medalist ice skater. Karl had been in the building for the World Circus Festival with his "comedy mule act," called by filmmaker Jacques Tati the funniest act in show business. It was an act with tradition, traced back to Mark Twain in Huckleberry Finn *(Chapter 23) and before that Dan Rice performing it for President Lincoln.*

I knew I could learn something about animals as well as comedy from Karl. And after the luxury of the circus building, I wanted more experience in shows under canvas.

After some time with the Hoffmans, he heads to France to study mime with Marcel Marceau.

Just before his truck and caravan pulled out, I stopped him. "Do you need any help next season?" He looked at me for a moment and then wrote down his address on a piece of scrap paper. "Can you be there first of March?" I nodded. "OK," he said, "see you down the road." Such is the way of circus business. A handshake and a nod, and business is done.

Rob spends a season performing with Karl Kossmayer and his Comedy Unrideable Mules. They start with the Hungarian Magyar State Cirkusz, traveling through Holland, Germany and Scandinavia, and end up with Cirkus Scott, a venerable Swedish circus traversing the entire country, even entertaining Laplanders far above the Arctic Circle. The premise of the act is simple. The music begins and a mule trots nonchalantly around the ring as volunteers from the audience attempt to ride him one at a time. As it happens, they can barely catch the mule, let alone jump on. Rob's job is to act like one of the audience volunteers and make sure the action is fast and nonstop—taking falls, getting kicked, jumping on and being thrown off with somersaults in the air, landing on his back in the sawdust, running for safety as the mule chases him trying to bite his rear end.

Kossmayer is also planted in the audience. A bald, meek-looking Everyman, he climbs into the ring chased by his fussing wife—he is so plain and unassuming that most of the audience figure he's just one of them. He and Rob gang up on the charging mule. They always lose. Rob gets chased into the audience and the mule pulls Kossmayer's pants down around his ankles in mid-flight. Even at the end, the audience never knows for certain that they're shills. A Dutch circus enthusiast later described Kossmayer's act as "a masterpiece on the border between fiction and reality...this little character carried to the ring a perfect history of the universal retired middle-class type, life dominated by his wife's discipline, wasting in a few seconds all his life's boring dignity to reach the impossible world of the clowns."

What fun, being battered and bruised twice daily for eight months! Darn mule. He was always testing me.

He was smart and sassy, but also gentle out of the ring. We gave kids rides on his back after the show. Once, in the middle of Stockholm during a morning training session for a new clown mule act, he eyed the ring exit, glanced at me, and I'd swear he winked. Then he took off out of the tent into the streets of the city!

Kossmayer yelled at me, "Go, Go, GO!" and I chased that mule through the city streets while wearing clown shoes and baggy pants. It is quite difficult to run while wearing clown shoes. He would stop a half block away to see if I was coming, wait for me, then take off again.

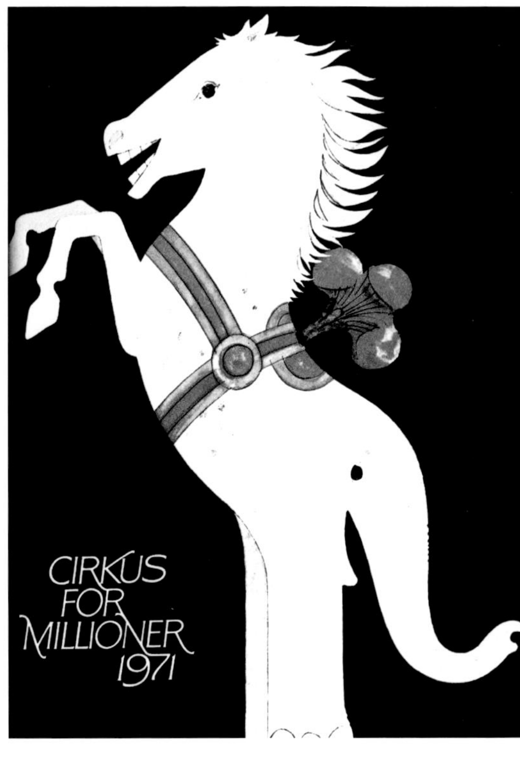

CIRCUS
STAR - TIME
CIRKUSBYGNINGEN

Left: Rob and Kansas the Mule.
Below: Rob's Italian clown mentors, The Francescos.

Idle spectators on the sidewalks, old ladies with shopping bags, men in suits, were startled to see a mule flash past followed by a half-dressed clown, so they left what they were doing for a more immediate spectacle and followed us to see how this could possibly play out. Several police got into the back end of the parade waving their sticks and yelling for me to Stop That Mule! Crowds cheered, cars honked in delight and Stockholm was jubilant. Two hours later I returned, exhausted, leading the fugitive back to the Big Top. I swear he was grinning. It was embarrassingly clear who was the biggest jackass.

There were misadventures APLENTY

Circus star time

BENNEWEIS

In time, Rob's stint with Kossmayer comes to an end. There are other shows, large and small, and galas in the capitals of Europe. He gets work for a couple of years as a regular cast member on a Danish hit TV series where he and his dog Rufus, a soulful clown with four legs, become celebrities. But even this begins to pale compared to the dream brewing inside him, of creating his own circus. It's time to return home.

The Hoffmans, Benneweis and Kossmayer have left their marks, though. And they will all jostle their way into the little Vermont circus that Rob doesn't yet know how he's going to create. Apprenticeship over.

Cleaning up after the soap gag, Copenhagen, 1974

CHAPTER TWO

GOING OUT UNDER CANVAS

Vermont's Own

Homegrown Country Circus

ROLL
TAKE
PROD. NO.
SCENE
SOUND
DATE
PROD. CO.
DIRECTOR
CAMERAMAN

That first circus introduced me to the town. I turned to teaching mime, wire walking and juggling to local farm kids in the farmhouse. I started a silent-film series in the horse barn. The old farmers came out for that, thanking me with tears in their eyes as they told stories of laughing at Chaplin as kids in the 1920s. I was paid for all these events in homemade jams, jars of pickled vegetables and firewood to get through the winter.

Winters were spent doing shows for schools with my dog, Rufus. Every morning I had to thaw the poor dog's frozen water bowl in the uninsulated kitchen, and tried to catch a glimpse of the sleek and playful weasel who sometimes peeked out from behind the couch. I called him Hermin, Mermin's Ermine. Snow piled as high as the front porch gutter.

In the spring thaw, after months of frozen water pipes, I took showers off the porch drain spouts whenever it rained. Thunder found me excitedly running for a bar of soap and stripping down.

I stared back at the cows who always got loose from the neighbor's farm to wander up and stare placidly in my windows. How the heck was I going to start a circus? With performing cows?

There's one practical thing a small-town traveling circus needs to get going: a tent. On visits to Tampa to work with his friend Stewart Lippe, Rob would go tent-shopping—"Some people buy clothes or cars," Stewart would laugh, "but your weakness is tent-shopping!" In the winter of 1986, with the help of family and friends, Rob designed and bought a small two-mast big top, a blue, green and yellow beauty that could seat 500 paying audience members. Rolled up in three huge canvas bags, it hibernated through the winter in the old horse barn, like three bears curled up in a cave.

His plan was to start a small professional show, get a reputation touring it around the state, then after a couple of years start teaching kids. It would be a detour on the road to a youth circus, he figured, but a necessary one. It was called The Green Mountain Circus, and he began hiring acts, booking the show to fire departments and town recreation departments as a fundraiser, and laying out funds for the upcoming tour. He had posters designed showing barnyard animals—pigs, ducks, cows—having fun in a circus ring. In all, 10 towns around Vermont signed up.

But the circus didn't get to a single one of them. That spring, 1986, the American insurance industry went haywire. The cost of liability insurance skyrocketed and, in the words of *The New York Times*, forced "cutbacks in the operations of everything from school districts and local governments to bowling alleys and day care centers." It could have added parks, recreation departments and anyone who might have planned to present a circus. Regretfully, all Rob's presenters canceled. He emptied his pockets to pay off his contracts with perform-

The larger feeling of Circus Smirkus is joyful, exuberant... Mostly, one remembers the applause echoing off the tent walls: loud, happy, foot-stomping applause.

—The New York Times, 1987

During that meal, Jay had asked me what I really wanted to do. I said it was a professional circus with youth, something entirely unique and with a charm that could only come from kids. That conversation with Jay made me realize my plan for The Green Mountain Circus was all wrong. I really wanted Circus Smirkus. The lesson here was a big one: don't compromise the dream.

It was a daunting task, living in the backwoods with no money, to establish not only a circus but a training ground in the seven months before summer. We had to work out contracts, insurance, auditions, staffing, housing, set design, trucks, touring logistics, public relations, marketing, bookings, sponsors and a nightmare of legal codes for everything concerning kids and circuses. And figure out how we'd actually take a group of essentially unskilled kids and turn them into a circus troupe. That turned out to be the easy part.

Jay recruited actor Donny Osman to help out. Director of the Governor's Institute on the Arts and founder of the Two Penny Theater, which in the '70s was New England's premier traveling commedia dell'arte *troupe, Donny made for a perfect ringmaster—energetic, enthusiastic, quick with one-liners, an exuberant wisecracker. I lined up Stewart, a longtime acquaintance who was a multi-skilled variety artist, documentary filmmaker and founder of The Franzini Family Circus, a traveling stage company from Florida. He could teach juggling and tightwire—along with knife-throwing, fire-eating and other esoteric sideshow skills probably unseen in the hills of Vermont for a hundred years. From New York, Karen Gersch and Barbie Rhind, known as The Acrobrats, came up to teach acrobatics and aerials (the second year, Nikki Swarthout replaced Barbie). I rounded out the coaching crew as artistic director and clown. Then we added Peter Tavalin, a composer and keyboardist, and two other musicians. This circus was going to have original live music!*

For his part, Jay lent the resources of Catamount Arts. He tapped into his

Why Circus?

The very idea of circus is something that needs to be practiced more extensively. A place where adults can bring kids together to reach beyond their grasp is transformative. There aren't many places where adults in an audience are looking at kids with genuine respect, awe and appreciation for what they've truly accomplished. We all go to our kids' recitals in fifth grade and applaud just for their willingness. But with circus you're seeing kids who are reaching beyond their grasp, achieving their dreams and achieving excellence. They're part of an ensemble where they have equal standing and make bonds and connections, genuinely engage with mentors, and find their own voices. That idea is profound and essential.
—Jay Craven

Why a Kids' Circus?

I'm asked why I started a circus with kids. I was very impressed by the maturity of the children of professional circus artists I worked with in Europe. Growing up in the world of circus seemed to impart an education in life missing from normal schooling. Circus kids understood geography and spoke several languages by necessity. Tolerance of other cultures was ingrained. Every day featured hard work, self-reliance, communal living and close-knit family life. I wanted to give American kids a taste of the same experiences. —Rob Mermin

fundraising network and enlisted crew members who'd worked with Catamount on earlier productions. He called town clerks around the state to see where a circus might be able to set up a 500-person tent. He sent out word to parents who'd been involved with Catamount projects to see if any had kids who might want to join up. Friends from around the region showed up to serve meals, work as counselors, sign on as roustabouts, dispense bandages and advice. We gave them all a chance to run away with the circus.

In the end, 50 kids applied to our two-week session. We took 15.

The kids came from all over... well, all over Vermont, anyway. To get in, they'd had to show what they could do, which wasn't much: a few could ride unicycles, some knew tumbling from their gymnastics training, there were a handful of jugglers. Mostly, Rob, Donny and Stewart wanted an inner spark, some sort of presence, a sense of fun. At the group audition, they peppered the kids with increasingly outlandish questions about how hard they were willing to work—would they do the dishes and clean toilets? For juggler Toby Ayer, a sober 12-year-old who couldn't make it to the tryout, Donny auditioned him by holding a conversation in gibberish.

The new troupers and their coaches had a week to put a show together. So they plunged into forward rolls and cartwheels, tightwire and pyramids, juggling and unicycle. They learned to stretch, did exercises to build their strength and got lectures in the fine points of clowning and slapstick timing. In the afternoon there was volleyball and Ping-Pong to let off steam. In the evening Rob and Stewart showed Chaplin, Keaton and Laurel & Hardy films, standing by the screen and expounding on lesson-worthy moments, or had the troupers watch Bugs Bunny, Road Runner and other cartoons, pointing out how the characters' extreme expressions distilled surprise and fear. Rob would read them a short story, after which the kids tumbled into bed, the four girls in bunks in the house, the boys relegated to an army tent borrowed from the National Guard in Burlington. It was exhausting work. As 12-year-old Pasquale DeMaio told a curious reporter, he'd never actually dreamed about running away to the circus, "but after coming here, I've dreamed of running away *from* the circus."

No one knew what to expect on opening night. Word had gotten out, and The Boston Globe *and Marialisa Calta from* The New York Times *were there. But even after they'd arrived, we had no idea whether anyone would actually show up. Everyone was nervous, running around at the last minute, fiddling with equipment, yelling for this costume or that prop.*

There hadn't been enough rehearsal time and the coaches were nervous. Composer Peter Tavalin was still working out all the bits for his original music. The novice

Top: Robbo and Rufus, Lippo and Bo.
Above: Robbo and Lippo.

Stewart could teach juggling and tightwire—along with knife-throwing, fire-eating and other esoteric sideshow skills...

staff was trying to figure out lighting cues and how to make the cotton candy machine work. Excited troupers put on the wrong costumes. Still, I knew we would surprise everyone, including ourselves, by putting on a "traditional" show, combining young troupers with the professionals: Donny in ringmaster's top hat, Lippo and Robbo as clowns alongside the novice clown alley of kids, Karen and Barbie doing their comedy routines. The show format and style were created that first year.

But a half hour before showtime, we were still just a fledgling circus troupe with a tent standing alone in a field and a couple of antsy reporters waiting to see what would happen. Then, suddenly, a car emerged out of the woods and came slowly up the road looking for a place to park. "OK," I thought. "We'll do the circus for one family." Then another car drove up, and then another and another, until there was an endless steel chain and it seemed as if the entire town of Greensboro was parked in the cow field near the tent.

I was exhausted and nervous, but ready for anything. I was familiar with circus chaos; the rest of the staff seemed not to have the foggiest idea of what we were about to pull off. As soon as the show started, you could feel the energy. Donny turned to me and said, "This place is electric! This is something really big!"

But the real stunner for me was the unexpected response after the show. I was overwhelmed with congratulations from one and all, assuring me that I must be triumphantly gratified to have reached "a dream come true." The only truth I knew was that we had somehow survived the night, but that the hard work of a tour hadn't even begun. As I shook hands all around, I was anxiously looking over my shoulders, eager to get back to work: that prop truck was not getting packed properly; the bleachers needed stacking; the tent....

The best comment of all came from my Uncle Harry, whose daughter Annie, my cousin, had come up to work as a counselor. He was a tall, thin, white-haired and patrician figure. He knew the long years of effort I'd put into trying to create a circus. So he waited for everyone else to finish with the congratulations, then put his hand on my shoulder, looked down at me solemnly, and in a stentorian voice announced, "'Tis comparable to the miracles that Moses wrought!"

Miracle, indeed. In 10 shows over six days, Smirkus drew enthusiastic crowds at three sites—Greensboro, Newport and Montpelier—and admiring attention from the *Times*, the *Globe*, numerous local papers and even some national circus publications. The acts were high-spirited: plate-spinning, audience members dancing in the ring, a magic metamorphosis box, acrobatics, Stewart juggling and presenting his tightrope-walking—and very real—boa constrictor, Barbie and Karen on the trapeze, Rob doing bubble magic. Determined to carry

Fireflies

At least one week every June, during rehearsal period, a nighttime walk is essential. The fireflies gather around the circus tent, which is set below the hayfield and near a beaver pond. They fill the valley in the millions, surrounding the tent and spreading up the hill until they meet the sea of stars like two sparkling rivers converging by moonlight. It is compelling enchantment. Your pulse begins beating to the rhythm of the staccato flashes of light, an almost deafening symphony of silence. You stand in the midst of acres of firestars, the tent glowing, the twinkling sky of stars blending with the winking and blinking fireflies, an infinite dance of sparks. There is no telling where the hill and field have gone or where space begins: the vast border separating sky and earth is gone. You are, for a time, among the stars on earth.

—Rob Mermin

PROGRAM
JAMAICA
ST. CROIX

on the long circus tradition of using live animals in a show, Rob had connected with a local llama farm—the owner came to every show so the troupers could do an animal walk-around in the ring and to provide rides before and after the show. Donny presided over it all as ringmaster with Brooklyn-accented flair. "Ever since man discovered reality, he's been trying to escape from it!" he announced as the magic box act was set to begin. "You're thinking that what you're about to see is nothing but a cheap circus trick. Let me tell you: It's an *expensive* circus trick!"

"I learned that if I really want to do something, with hard work I can achieve it. No star is out of reach."

—Kaleen McKeeman,
former trouper, now circus professional

jitters!
before opening night, year 1

From counselor Annie Klein's Journal

Crisis No. 7: Kids and parents arrive today. The stove broke down (from nervous tension?) so another was brought in, but didn't fit through the front door. Lots of discussion; it was dismantled (the door)... meanwhile the overloaded fridge shuddered and stopped, in sympathetic protest.

No. 14 (July 4): Full house, 50 circus people and kids—plumbing decides to back up, toilets everywhere overflow. Lots of scurrying and the cook is digging outside with a shovel. Lots of jokes. Septic truck finally arrives with American flag waving on the hood, more jokes. It's a happy stinky Fourth of July.

No. 15: Skunko, the friendly critter living under the barn, came out to watch the septic proceedings, was appalled at the chaos (or the stink), sprayed his emotions and left. Show opens in three days.

No. 19: The health inspector on a surprise visit, stone-faced, taking notes in the kitchen... Molly runs in barefoot, happily holding up a garden snake and offers it to the cook who is making stew.

No. 20: Rob can be seen holidng his head in his hands, looking around, groaning.

No. 28: Rob should be at rehearsals, but power went out... He is at the house in the basement, fooling with the fuse box. No lights in house, tent, barn.

No. 29: Reporter and photographer arrive from **New York Times**.

No. 30: Opening is two days away.

General note: Donny is heard with his daily cry, "Year One! Year One!" in reassurance (to himself?) that we are learning, we are learning... Stewart arrives at tent with phone message from Dottie, Rob's mom: "Tell him to stop all this nonsense and get a job in a bank!"

Circus Smirkus will be in the annals of American circus history.
The troupers, bursting through the routines, were the heart of the show.

—Boston Globe, 1987

NORTHERN LIGHTS

After the opening night in July '87,
as the audience wandered home and the crew and
troupers began the tent take-down, the night sky started
changing colors and gave us a midnight show.

Shadowy white clouds were slowly painted pink in the
north sky over the Circus Barn and fields.
Gigantic streaks of white and red and deep
night-blue grew in slow motion like outstretched fingers
across the full heavenly panorama.
The monstrous hand was shimmering,
slowly shifting, so huge and numinous you had to stop
staring and look down for a moment, then back up to
notice the subtle changes.

The aurora borealis was blessing the maiden voyage
of our little Big Top.

—Rob Mermin

Circus Mom

My mother, Dottie, was a private person, content to be out of the spotlight in family iife. On the last show of the first Smirkus year she came and sat unobtrusively in the center section of bleachers. When I took the microphone at the finale to thank the audience for coming, I announced there was a special guest in the house: "My mother!!" The spotlight went to her and caught her by surprise. As the audience applauded enthusiastically, she sat there mortified. I grinned happily.

The second year, my mother came to the show and quietly took her seat. I announced a special guest: "My mother!!" She sat there accepting the applause, gently nodding her head a few times, ill at ease with the whole thing.

The third year, I told the troupe to be ready to run out throwing confetti and go up and surround my mom with hugs, as the band played happily. But she got the jump on us! When I announced her she promptly stood up, smiling broadly, waving to the audience all around like a seasoned celebrity!

That's when I knew she finally accepted the idea that her son was in the circus business. In the following years she hosted hordes of Russians, Mongolians, Latvians and other foreign guests sleeping on the floor of her tiny house in Connecticut as a stopover on their way from the New York airport up to Smirkus. They still talk about the Circus Mom making pancakes and blintzes for breakfast on their first morning in America. —Rob Mermin

CHAPTER THREE

A LITTLE TENT IN THE WOODS

Misadventures of a Ragtag Company in the Northeast Kingdom

Overheard in the days before cell phones and e-mail:
Mom: "Call us when something exciting happens."
Trouper: "But Mom, every day something exciting happens!"

A MEMO to STAFF from Rob Mermin

We aim to project fun, optimism, hopefulness, dedication, playfulness, whimsy, warmth, caring, authenticity, inspiration, energy, unabashed sentiment, genuine emotion, gentle humor, outright silliness and generosity of spirit. Our broader goal is to create delight, compel wonder, expand amazement, invite enchantment, spread joy, evoke childhood, nourish dreams, activate imagination, trigger inspiration, propel adventures and have fun. Laughter is our hard currency.

What may have been most miraculous about Smirkus wasn't that it pulled off a few shows its first year. It was that it turned around and did it again the next summer, putting on 28 shows in 11 Vermont towns over three weeks. And then it got even more ambitious: in 1989, *Running Home to the Circus* made it beyond Vermont's borders, touching down in New Hampshire and Massachusetts as well.

"Tentman Dave" from Tampa built the little big top and was the first Smirkus tent boss. He could be found every evening up the hill sitting by a campfire smoking his pipe, like some gnome that had come out at night from the woods. Scrawny, scruffy and laconic, he could swing a 20-pound sledgehammer one-handed.

Up in Newport, Vermont, Stewart accidentally backed the van he was living in into Lake Memphremagog (when the company showed up the next year, there was a sign planted in the water just offshore: "Reserved for Mr. Lippe"); one of the guys hanging around who

The hard life of being on the road...

helped him pull it out was a brawny, tattooed, long-haired nightclub bouncer named Chris Butler, who immediately signed on to the tent crew and ended up spending the next 10 summers pounding stakes, hauling canvas, setting up sound and lights, and—to the befuddlement of everyone who knew him back home—good-naturedly chaperoning little kids. Irina Gold, a former Russian Olympic gymnast and consultant to the Big Apple Circus, joined up as a coach; "a walking muscle," as early counselor Barb Baird calls her, she gave Smirkus its first taste of the tough-minded dedication that Russians and other classically trained Easterners bring to their art. Ozzie Henchel, who'd known Rob casually as a child in Connecticut and had worked with Jay on productions at Catamount Arts, helped out with the tent, carpentry and other odd jobs—until in 1993 he became Smirkus's tour manager, all-around Mr. Fixit and resident wise uncle.

It wasn't only staff or crew who felt pulled by the spirit taking hold on the old farm. When Stewart, Rob or one of the other coaches had an idea for an act that needed some piece of serious apparatus, they would head over to a welder in Greensboro Bend who could turn the idea into solid reality—a trapeze bar, a climbing pole, whatever they needed. "We were inventing this stuff as we went along," Stewart recalls. "There weren't places to buy it. Everyone around knew what we were doing, and was supportive. There was a sense that the community was looking out for us too."

This might have been because circus acts and the apparatus to go with them weren't the only thing Rob and his compatriots were inventing as they went along. The whole thing was. There was no manual: not on how to create acts; or to build skills so the acts could get better; or to deal with high-spirited and, pretty much by definition, unusual teenagers; or to have them help put a show together and take it on the road to towns that hadn't seen a circus drop by for half a century; or to craft a style, spirit and philosophy that would carry it not just from one town to the next, but from one year to the next.

I knew exactly what I wanted. My dream was to bring the best traditions of European circus to American kids: the hard life of being on the road mixed with a grand spirit of adventure. It was to be a revival of the tradition of small tent circuses—the mud shows—traveling to rural villages that the larger shows no longer played. It was to be a place where experienced circus artists worked as colleagues with talented students, in an atmosphere where the discipline, customs, traditions and lifestyle of the itinerant circus were respected and passed on. It was to be a one-ring show with the artistic style of classical European circus and exuberant American energy and slapstick spirit.

mixed with a grand spirit of adventure.

What I had learned from the Hoffmans is that you have to earn your way into the circus world—pay your dues, endure the tests and show that as an outsider you have a feel for the sawdust. You have to be self-reliant and ready for anything that life on the road and in a circus tent can throw at you. And while not all circus performers have the luxury of working in Europe's circus palaces, I came away from those experiences with a sense of the artistry, style and class of traditional circus. Smirkus would strive—as do circus artists all over the world—to show just how far humans can reach when the spirit wants to fly.

Our philosophy relied on the notion that people of diverse backgrounds and personalities can get along without malice, that young people are eager to contribute the best of themselves to the world and that hard work and communal effort can produce joy. It was an embarrassingly simple ideal.

Jay Flies

At the end of the second year's tour, Jay bowed out of Smirkus, leaving it to the umbrella organization Rob had created, The Circus Barn, Inc. Though there was tension between the two men at the time, Jay credits Smirkus with giving him the confidence to become a feature filmmaker. "The circus," he says, "was a very good warmup for me in terms of the producing skills that were needed to work with large numbers of people, keep them pointed in the same direction, and deal with a range of temperaments—including artistic temperaments—in building a team."

"When I think of Smirkus, I don't think of being on the road, I think of spending my time at the barn. It was the first place I felt the family of Smirkus. The bell at mealtimes, going to council meetings, playing Ping-Pong, feeling the floor of the studio teeter up and down as we did jumping jacks, sneaking into the pantry in the middle of the night with Tamir to steal Oreos... I know that place like the back of my hand—I know all the secret stairways, the passages, the shortcuts to cut people off. We explored that place from the roof to the basement."

—Patrick Mannion,
former Smirko, now chef and circus performer

Kids slept in the barn, in barely converted horse stalls with sheets as doors, though some of the younger girls got bunks in the cramped rooms that lined the hall between the house and the barn. All the buildings—the barn, the farmhouse, the various sheds—had the worn, creaky look of centuries of hard use. Even after troupers moved out of their horse stalls and began sleeping in the three "rustic" trailers that make up the corner known as "Trailerville," the whole place announced that creature comforts came second. This was circus. And rural Vermont. You made do.

Yet starting with the first year's troupers, generations of Smirkos made "the Barn," as they call the entire enclave, home. "The house was our house," says Toby Ayer, a first-year trouper who became a Smirkus mainstay and an eventual Rhodes scholar. "The living room was our living room. The kitchen was our kitchen. The place became part of you."

They woke up early—in the first year to the sound of Rob in his pajamas playing Bach on his trumpet, and later to counselor Jacob Edgar's trumpet versions of Beatles songs—and stumbled out to communal breakfasts under a tent. They went to bed late, after nighttime snack and short stories or ghost stories or circus stories or Chaplin films or, one summer, watching Jacob act out *The Princess Bride* as he read it cover to cover. They hung out in the living room paging through Rob's collection of old circus books and memorabilia, losing themselves in the pictures and stories about this strange world on whose threshold they stood.

"Days at Smirkus are more beautiful than just about any day anywhere," says Casey Pickett, a first-generation trouper. "The fields, the blue sky, the house and the barn...and this sense of unbelievable possibility."

It was as though, once you popped out of the woods along Circus Road and got to the barn, you'd entered another world. There was a single television with bad reception, no Internet and just one telephone for troupers to use. Away from the cares of ordinary life—the in-crowds, the siren call of pop culture, the homework and teachers and parents and classmates—kids found room to be themselves. "You know how you might get back to school in September and there's going to be cliques and bullies and all that stuff you have to deal with?" Ozzie would tell them right after they arrived. "We don't have that here. Forget about that stuff and breathe easy, because it ain't happening here!" Each new season was an improvisation in circus and an impromptu lesson in how to deal with kids and teenagers. Rob, Stewart and Donny believed that, as Rob put it, "When you give young people the authority and responsibility to achieve the goals that inspire them, the hard work and self-discipline necessary to achieve success will be there."

So from the beginning kids did daily chores: washing dishes, scrubbing pots and pans, taking out compost, sweeping the house and barn. They learned to pound stakes with the tent crew, set up bleachers and ring curbs, arrange and care for props, sweep the ring. Each evening, everyone would gather for Council Meetings, which took place in the studio after dinner chores—and in the circus ring once they were out on tour—and talk about

Troupers and crew, 1988

"Everyone in the circus is accepted, but Smirkus has some magic that brings those kids closer, faster than I have ever seen any group become one unit."

—Chris Combs, father of clown Ryan Combs

whatever needed discussing, from bedtimes to personal problems to chores to the show itself. They would vote on matters of policy and explore what it took to survive such close living and working conditions.

Molly Saudek, who arrived in 1988 and is now an internationally known wire-dancer, remembers the feeling those early years instilled. "We had no bedtimes, but if there was a problem and kids showed up at practice sleepy or were keeping people up with noise, then it was brought up in council meetings, with kids discussing it and deciding on consequences. Kids took great responsibility for themselves: it was clear that if you showed up without having slept you couldn't do good work, and everyone wanted to do good work. Instead of having a list of rules that we had to follow, we developed a sense of responsibility to the community."

Skunko

You agree when you join Smirkus that you're not going to bring candy, gum or junk food with you. But one summer night, I had this Trident gum next to the bunk where I was sleeping. Suddenly, I woke up to rustling. "Chris!" It was Jade, who was in the next bunk over. "Chris!" he said. "Don't move!" And suddenly I see, there on my chest, wagging its tail in my face, there's this skunk. He's chewing my bubble gum! So what do you do? I stayed very still, and when he scampered off I flew out of that bunk, over the wooden beams, and landed in Jade's bunk. And that's where I stayed the rest of the night. When I went back to my bunk in the morning to straighten up, there were all these Trident wrappers in it. And that's why you don't sleep with candy next to you in the bunk.

—Chris Grabher, 10 years old at the time

Circus Road

One year, an official green road sign appeared at the end of the dirt road. In those days, no road in Greensboro had a sign; few of the roads in town even had names. Then the state decreed that every street and back road needed a name for 911 purposes. It was a total surprise—and honor—to discover that town officials had named us Circus Road. A hundred years from now, some old farmer will be telling tall tales about why there's a backwoods road called Circus Road. I'd love to eavesdrop on that conversation! —Rob Mermin

Henrietta in the Barn

There were always noises at night in the barn. Sometimes you'd be up in the studio practicing and hear heavy footsteps below, stick your head down to see who it was, and no one would be there.We were talking about this over dinner one night, and Rob said, "Oh, that's just Henrietta." We were confused. There were no troupers or staff named Henrietta. Rob told us that half a century ago the former owners had a horse named Henrietta. She plowed fields, pulled timber in from the forest and slept in the barn at night. When he was living in the barn by himself he would hear the noises as well, and suggested that we talk to her, that she was a friendly spirit who had just stayed in her home past her time. From that day on, every time we heard something that would normally make us nervous, we would know that it was Henrietta, swishing her tail or moving her feet. Once Rob told us the story that year, Henrietta's Ghost Story became a mainstay, spookier each year. We'd have a sleepover in the studio, and Rob would sit there with a flashlight under his chin and tell us how in the middle of winter once, he heard horse clip-clops outside. When he went out to check there were horse prints in the snow from the barn headed down the road and up the hill. He followed them. And halfway up the hill, they faded away... —Francey Grund

The Smirkus style in the ring—of charm, playfulness, joyfulness and respect for the audience—developed over time, but its essence was there from early on. We believed that each trouper should get a well-rounded education in the liberal circus arts, and that they needed to experience the satisfaction and dignity inherent in studying and mastering a craft.

So we immersed them in a wide variety of circus skills, from juggling to tumbling to pyramids to wire-walking to trapeze and other aerials. They needed to get a firm foundation of the circus arts, before specializing in one act.

Even more important, they had to learn the circus lifestyle by living it. It's an itinerant lifestyle, demanding self-discipline and responsibility to one another. A circus allows no idle hands. We expected them to do ring and tent chores not just because they had to get done, but to learn how to live as an artist and not a prima donna. It's hard to be an elitist performer when you're hauling bleachers and picking up trash after the show.

And because everyone in a small circus depends on everyone else to make it down the road, they had to learn rigging, prop maintenance and how the tent went up and got taken down. Just as important, we wanted them to learn circus history, so that they had an appreciation not just of the world they were entering, but of the skill, perseverance and creativity of the generations of performers, impresarios and crew who'd come before them. Circus is a global subculture, with its own customs, lingo, superstitions, history and traditions. Every generation of young Smirkus troupers has chosen to step into the ring and become part of that exclusive world. The cultural history and traditions must be passed on.

As Rob and Stewart taught clowning or juggling, they never just taught a trick—they also told stories about where it had come from, who'd performed it and what variations others before them had invented. They taught mime or pratfalls, but they also taught the psychology behind them: why this move or that, and in what order, would make the audience laugh.

By hanging out with Rob, Stewart and the other coaches, kids learned almost by osmosis. The young troupers began to learn that what set their experience apart from camp wasn't just the skills they were learning or even the audiences they were entertaining. It was that the show—and Smirkus itself—depended on them.

What Smirkus was teaching, in other words, wasn't just particular circus skills. It was a way of life and, even more important, a way of looking at life. Take what you were learning seriously, but don't take yourself too seriously. Learn the discipline it takes to perform to the best of your abilities, but be sure you make time for fun. Be a close-knit family, but in the ring make sure you welcome the audience as respected guests. "It was essential—and natural—in the beginning," says Rob, "to treat the kids not just as students, but as colleagues in this effort. It was their circus."

Passing the Torch

In 2005, Molly Saudek came back to Smirkus to coach the wire act. Working several times each day with a new generation of wire walkers—Abby Suskin, Patrick "P.T." Tobin, Jacob "Green" Sherry and Jacob Bloom—she suddenly understood why, when she was a young trouper, coaches had become so attached to and lifelong friends with the young troupers in their charge: "It's because when you're working with kids that way, they seem not like kids. You share a goal of putting out something that's polished and finished, where you know you're taking risks and pushing yourselves. Kids put away their pettiness and competitiveness and worries about looks or being cool; they put all that aside when there's a clearly defined creative and physical challenge in front of them. Working with them daily on that, you don't see them as kids, but as full-blown human beings. That was the first time I appreciated how it was that Rob, Donny and Stewart could keep the feeling we had early on that everyone's on an equal footing: kids will give you back that adultness and focus and ability to function as a voting member of society."

"After a full day of training I'd walk down to the main tent, the Chapiteau, *with a friend. It would be night, with lightning bugs all around, and we'd pull a crash mat into the middle of the ring and lie down on it and look up. There are stars on the ceiling of the tent, and in the dark it felt like you were almost touching the canopy of the universe—you were that close to the edge of the stars."*

—Kerren McKeeman, former trouper, now circus performer

"At Smirkus you're so free. You have nothing else to worry about than to be creative and do good shows, and you reach this level where your brain doesn't think about 'No' at all, it just thinks about 'Yes.' All this creative energy is flowing out without any mental block. That kind of environment is really hard to find out in the world."

—Sam Brown,
former trouper, now a circus performer

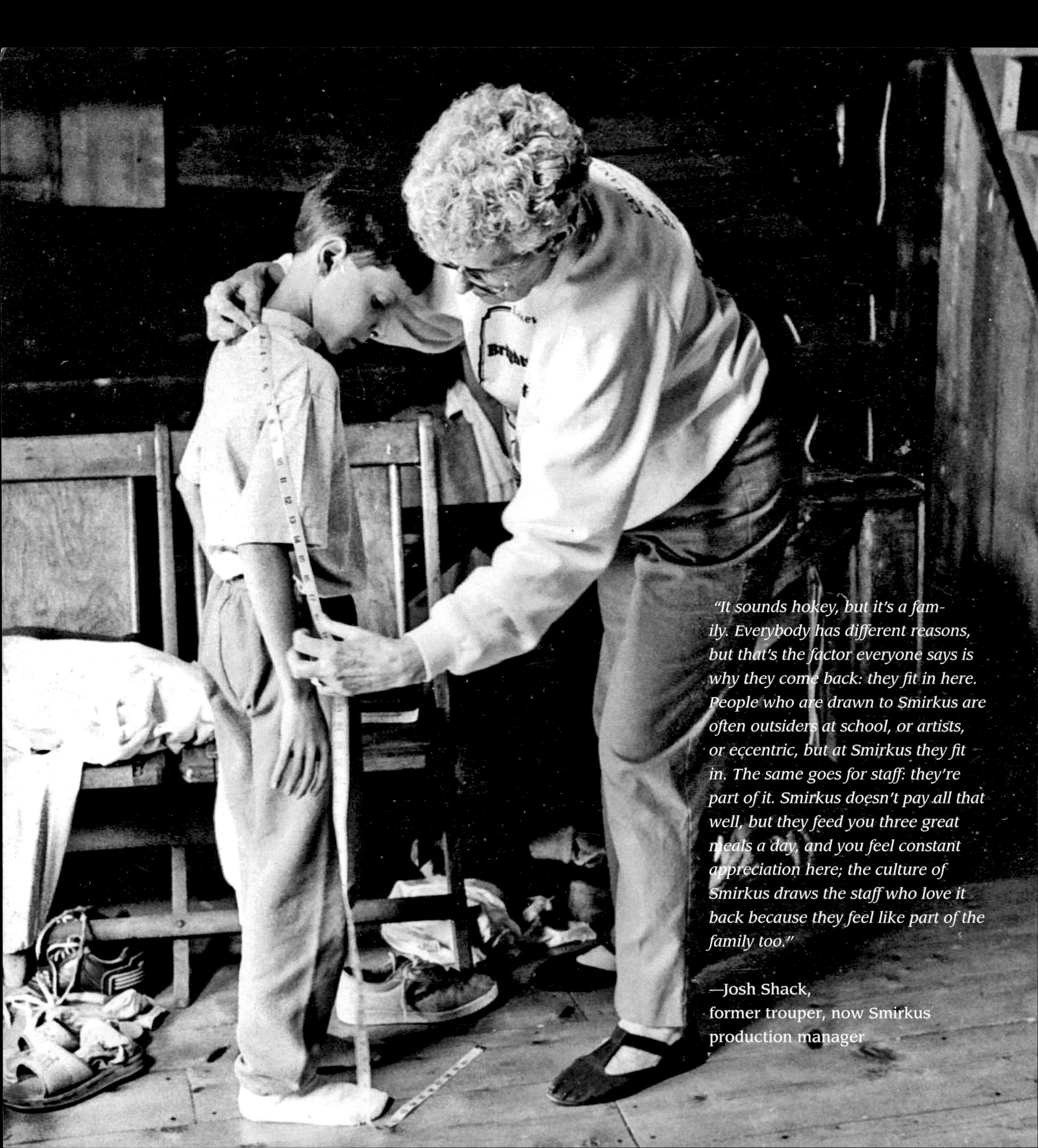

"It sounds hokey, but it's a family. Everybody has different reasons, but that's the factor everyone says is why they come back: they fit in here. People who are drawn to Smirkus are often outsiders at school, or artists, or eccentric, but at Smirkus they fit in. The same goes for staff: they're part of it. Smirkus doesn't pay all that well, but they feed you three great meals a day, and you feel constant appreciation here; the culture of Smirkus draws the staff who love it back because they feel like part of the family too."

—Josh Shack,
former trouper, now Smirkus production manager

SMIRKUS

SMIRKUS

Marÿn

The truest test of the Smirkus spirit and the generosity of youth came in the 1989 tour. Nothing else in Smirkus's history has matched it for either drama or tragedy.

That summer, Marÿn van der Vaart joined the troupe as a counselor. A circus enthusiast from Holland, 26 years old, she was touring the U.S. to make circus connections and ran across Stewart in Florida. With green eyes, a star-bright smile, an abiding love for kids and infectious enthusiasm, she made an immediate impression. Stewart called Rob. "I'm sending you your future wife!" he announced. Within days of arriving, she'd become a beloved member of the Smirkus family.

When Marÿn first stepped out of the car onto Vermont soil, our eyes met and my life—and the trajectory of Smirkus history—changed. On a rare day off in the middle of the tour, she and I took an afternoon swim alone at a secluded lake in Greensboro. As we sat on the shore our conversation turned to our dreams for a future together. She felt a renewal of spirit and confidence about the future, though, puzzling for her, she could not envision any of it. There was only a calm readiness for whatever lay ahead. We got back into the car...

Headed back to the Barn, Marÿn was driving, Rob and Rufus were in the passenger seat. On a washed-out part of the dirt road, the car suddenly veered off into a tree. Marÿn was killed instantly; Rufus appeared dead and Rob was lying in the road, his life dangling by a thread. An old farmer happened along about a half hour later and found them.

That afternoon the police arrived at the barn with the news. With Rob in the hospital and Rufus in the care of local vets, troupers and staff met in an emergency council meeting. Two shows were scheduled for the next day and they had to decide what to do.

The council was held, I am told, surrounding the large crystal boulder in the forest across the field from the barn. This was a sacred spot, a place to go when one needed solitude from the world. The young troupers made their decision: they wanted to perform in tribute to Marÿn, and to keep the circus alive for me. The emotions simply cannot be written.

"Rob created a show bigger than himself," Donny later said. "The show is bigger than one person." It fell to Donny and Stewart to rally the troupe, calm emotions and step into Rob's shoes as the focal point for troupers.

The first show after the accident was in Montpelier and the tent was filled with parents, friends of the circus and a few others who knew what had happened. They were heart-struck watching the young troupers' devotion. The general public had no idea of tragedy, only that they seemed to be witnessing an especially radiant show.

Jacob Edgar, a counselor, took over Rob's bubble act. "It was a dry, hot day and the bubbles weren't working, but his presence was fantastic—he connected immediately with the audience," remembers Porter Lontz-Underhill, who'd just joined Smirkus that summer as a trouper. "After the act, he left the ring, went behind the buses and just sobbed. It was heartbreaking to see. It was a beautiful show, and very painful. We didn't know what it was going to be like performing without Rob and then going home and not being tucked in by Marÿn. That performance showed us we could do it—that the show and life would go on."

Sudden tragedy is like a flash of lightning to the heart. I lay in the hospital able to move only my eyes. After 10 days the hospital sent me home, and I made it to the last show of the Smirkus tour. I took an aisle seat. The audience virtually disappeared; the troupers seemed to perform for no one else, all eye contact was directed at me. After each act the performers styled to the audience, then jumped the ring curb to give me a hug before jumping back and running through the curtain. I sat there and wept.

After the show I slowly made my way to the ring to give the traditional short speech to the company at the close of a season. How I managed this is a mystery, because when I returned to the hospital for a checkup three weeks later—over a month after the accident—the doctors discovered in a panic that the reason I was still moving stiffly, like a marionette without strings, was because I had been walking around with a broken neck.

CHAPTER FOUR

HEART AND SOUL

American Spirit and Russian Soul Bond Under the Big Top

> The Soviet/American Youth Circus: Even one year ago it was unthinkable. This deep connection happened here—without any tension or rivalry, but instead pure joy and friendliness.
>
> —Yaroslavl (Russia) newspaper, Spring 1990

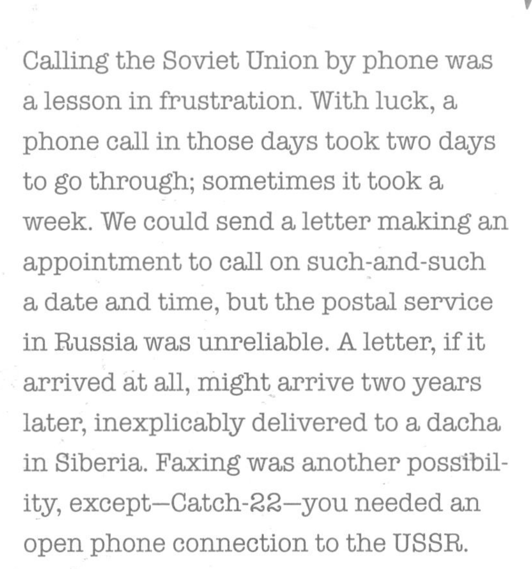

Dialing the USSR!

Calling the Soviet Union by phone was a lesson in frustration. With luck, a phone call in those days took two days to go through; sometimes it took a week. We could send a letter making an appointment to call on such-and-such a date and time, but the postal service in Russia was unreliable. A letter, if it arrived at all, might arrive two years later, inexplicably delivered to a dacha in Siberia. Faxing was another possibility, except—Catch-22—you needed an open phone connection to the USSR.

The best way to communicate was to corral some government official flying over and smuggle a letter in their diplomatic pouch. Charlie Hosford and Project Harmony were very helpful to us at this game.

You might have expected five broken ribs, a fractured elbow, a broken nose and a broken neck to temper Rob's ambitions a bit. Instead, they gave him time to think. Smirkus had been launched. It had attracted a loyal group of troupers committed to sticking with it and building their skills. It had won attention from *The New York Times, The Boston Globe, People* magazine and a pile of local newspapers. Towns on its route were clamoring for its return.

Still, it remained a ragtag group with more ambition than ability. It was ready to boost its artistic standards. What it really needed was an infusion of discipline and coaching talent. And the best place to find those, Rob knew, was in the Soviet Union, which produced some of the best circus performers in the world. That, he decided, was where he needed to look if he wanted to realize the dream he'd shared with Marÿn of an international youth circus.

"Soyuzgostsirk": An academy of...

In 1989, Smirkus had hosted a group of dancers from Tbilisi, Georgia. They had arrived courtesy of Project Harmony, a Vermont-based group that ran high school student exchanges with the Soviet Union. David Kelley, who along with Charlie Hosford had founded Project Harmony, was planning to go to Moscow that fall. So Rob wrote a letter to the director of the Moscow Circus proposing a cultural exchange and cooperative performances bringing together Soviet and American kids. Then he asked David to carry the letter with him, find someone connected to the Soviet circus and see that it got into the right hands.

It wasn't quite like sticking a message in a bottle, tossing it into the Atlantic and hoping it got to Moscow's Red Square. But it wasn't far off.

The Soviet circus bureaucracy was huge, a product of 70 years of a Communist system that considered circus to be the people's art and had created an entire world—training facilities, circus buildings, hotels, coaches, musicians, technicians, engineers—to hone

Alla Youdina, trapeze on ice.

and support its artists. Ever since 1919, when Lenin declared circus a national treasure—"an academy of physical beauty and merriment," as his first People's Minister of Education declared—circus had been nurtured as a refined public art in the Soviet Union in the same fashion as ballet and opera. The state circus company, *Soyuzgostsirk*, sent its 12,000 performers not only around the vast expanse of the Soviet Union, but all over the world. A letter from a tiny kids' circus in an obscure corner of the United States didn't stand a chance.

But here we need to pause for a moment and introduce a new character. Alla Youdina grew up in the Ural Mountains. At the age of 16, having trained in gymnastics and skating, and in technical school studying to be an electrical engineer, she heard that the Moscow Ballet on Ice was mounting a national search for new performers. She signed up for auditions.

It took three auditions—5,600 skaters, dancers and acrobats had come from all over the Soviet Union to compete for just a handful of slots—but eventually Alla joined 19 others in the new company. Only it turned out not to be a ballet on ice, but something entirely new: the first Moscow Circus on Ice. After two years of training from dawn until well into the night, the troupe was ready to open, and for the next seven years Alla performed all over the world—trapeze, Spanish web and dance, all on skates. She later joined *Soyuzgostsirk* as a top official running the division charged with designing and creating new acts in Soviet circuses and theaters. One evening in 1989... but let's let Alla tell the story:

physical beauty and merriment.

I had a good friend, and it was his wife's birthday party. My husband and I went, and we were sitting there, and the chair next to me was empty. "Who are you expecting?" I asked. "Oh," they told me, "we have a new friend from America. His name is David Kelley.' He eventually arrived. My English wasn't very good, so I didn't understand very much, but then he asked me what I did. I said that I did circus. He jumped up. "You do circus??!! Wait! I have a letter for you!" And he ran to his coat and got the letter. It was addressed to a

Mr. Sirotkin at the Moscow Circus. He said, "The director of a circus in America asked me to deliver this letter. Do you know this Mr. Sirotkin?"

I smiled and said, "Yes, I do. His office is next to mine." But then I had to explain that in our system, the KGB always had a man who traveled with the circus. Officially he was the "director" of the tour, but he actually had nothing to do with it; he was just KGB. That's who Rob had addressed his letter to! If I delivered it, it would have ended up in the garbage can.

Alla decided to take on the project herself and sent a fax to Rob inviting him to come discuss how to bring American kids to the Soviet Union. He booked a flight to Moscow and set about getting his visa. Then he waited. And waited. As the time for his flight approached, he put in panicked calls to Washington, checking on the visa. No one knew when it would get to him. The day of the flight arrived.

It was February, and very cold. I hopped on my flight without my visa. I had to change planes in Helsinki, and that's where I first ran into trouble. When I checked in for the flight to Moscow, the man at the desk told me I couldn't get into the country without a visa. I insisted that this was my problem, not his.

"When you get there they're just going to send you back," he said.

I shrugged. He sighed and waved me on. "Either they'll send you to Siberia," he said, "or I'll see you later tonight."

In Moscow, I stood in a long line. "Passport!" the stern-looking guard said when I finally got to the front. I slapped it down. "Visa!" he growled. I shook my head. He didn't look up. "Visa!" I shook my head again, and smiled. He called over another guard, and then a third one, this one with a rifle. This was beyond their experience. Other armed soldiers showed up, and after a lengthy discussion they marched me away—one on each side, another behind, all with rifles over their shoulders—and up some stairs to the security director's office.

The director of airport security was a big man with a barrel chest and no neck. We went through the same pantomime: Passport! Visa! I pointed to my bags, on which, with shrewd foresight, I had plastered circus stickers, including one with large Cyrillic letters: "Tsirk!" I said.

"Tsirk?"

"Da! Da! Da!" I said. "Klown!" I added, taking a pose. I knew that clowns were highly respected in the USSR.

"Prove it!" he pantomimed.

I picked up a stapler, an ashtray and one of the director's cigars from his desk and juggled them. He liked that. Then I started to hand back his cigar, but made it disappear. The soldiers with rifles liked that. I could tell the director was starting to soften.

Suddenly, he sat back and folded his arms. I stared back at him, with a little smile on my face. The time was right. "Skolko?" I asked. "How much?" He scribbled a figure on a scrap of paper: 50.

"Dollars? I asked. He nodded.

I took out $50 and put it on his desk. He pulled out a stamp, pounded it on a visa, and the guards escorted me to the street.

Alla Youdina,
Smirkus head coach, 1994

"I was at home that evening when the telephone rang. It was my friend Yuri —the friend whose apartment I'd met David Kelley in. Rob's letter had come in December, and it was only February—I hadn't expected him to come for a year. And he said, 'Somebody here knows you!' So I went to Yuri's house, right around the corner. He opened the door and Rob appeared. He said, 'Hi, I'm Rob Mermin from Circus Smirkus.'

What does all this say? It says it was meant to be! It was in the stars.

So we walked in the February snow to my house, and he had vodka with my family—we were up half the night, talking and laughing. The next day we wrote a letter of proposal, to bring Rob and Circus Smirkus to Moscow..."

—Alla Youdina

Rob and Alla at Budapest Circus Festival

But there was a problem. Rob had expected David Kelley to meet him, but he was nowhere to be found. Standing outside, flustered, he noticed some friends he'd made on the flight getting into a car headed for the city. Their friend, Yuri, obligingly took him along. Since Rob had nowhere to stay, Yuri agreed to take him home while they figured something out. Rob began his tale of woe—a phone call to Kelley's hotel revealed he was out of town—and wondered how to contact someone from the circus named Alla Youdina. Yuri interrupted. "Alla?!!" he shouted. "She's my neighbor!"

As exhilarating as all this was for Rob, his trip home a week later provided the exclamation point. Once again, he connected through Helsinki. The same agent he'd met on the way to Moscow was standing at the gate. He did a double take when he saw Rob. "You're back??!!" he exclaimed.

"Yes!" Rob said, enthusiastically. "Siberia was lovely!"

The next time Rob went to Moscow, it would have been harder to sneak in. Incredibly, barely three months after his visit to Moscow he was once again in the USSR, this time traveling with a dozen Smirkus troupers and a handful of coaches and chaperones.

For six days, the troupers got to know the circus world in Moscow. They stayed at the hotel maintained by *Soyuzgostsirk* for its performers, trained with budding young Soviet circus artists and were taken to circus performances at both the Old and the New Moscow Circus. They saw acts whose sheer artistry and technical mastery was unlike anything they'd experienced at home, including an entire half of a show performed in the circus ring filled with water, in which Volodya Avgustov—later to become a Smirkus coach—paddled a canoe while supporting on his forehead a 15-foot pole, on top of which balanced his wife, Zina. Afterward, they were taken backstage to meet the performers. "Now," Toby Ayer says, "we were connected to the real thing."

The whole experience was eye-opening. For most of the young Smirkos, it was the first glimpse of what it meant to take circus training seriously—and what the results could be. "That period of time, the '70s and '80s, it was the Great Depression of circus culture in the United States," says Jade Kindar-Martin, a key early trouper who went on to international fame as a high-wire walker. "And suddenly we find ourselves in a country where it's the national pastime."

"The old Moscow Circus," remembers Molly Saudek, "is this incredibly beautiful building, ornate, with this huge lobby, marble floors, big marbled pillars, and you go in and there's the ring and rows and rows of red velvet seats. The work you see there is the best circus in the world. Years before Cirque du Soleil, years before the new wave of circus in Europe, the Russians were doing the highest-quality technical work, but even beyond that they were looking into the philosophy that circus can express and how it's a metaphor for all of our great life triumphs."

Yet the breakdown of the Soviet system was apparent everywhere. That summer, the

command economy had managed to secure cherries—but they were pretty much the only fruit available. Even bars of soap were rationed. The Russian circus artists, with guile, perseverance and the courage born of a stoic history, managed to find a way of treating their visitors as honored guests. But even the American kids noticed that, while there was a bakery with fresh bread in the circus building, there were bread lines on the Moscow streets.

"That year when they came, we had very little food on the table," Alla remembers. "My family could afford to buy two apples and divide them in four, so that each of us would have half of an apple in front of us. There were no eggs for six months—in the entire country, no eggs! Bananas, peaches... for my boys, these were just things you read about in books. And there was no milk: The government only sold milk for children under two. If you were three or older, no milk for you. So we ate potatoes. Two apples for three days. We could afford four plums. I bought by the number, not the pound. So imagine the challenge of trying to feed American children!"

This wasn't the only challenge. So was the fact that while the Soviet hosts knew what their plans for the Americans were, they didn't really know how to communicate them. The Americans were left mostly in the dark.

Eventually, we left Moscow on a chartered bus heading north to the city of Yaroslavl on the Volga River. It was a company of new friends: Russian kids, American kids, coaches, reporters, KGB. We understood there was a circus building there, available for our use for a few days. It was an exciting thought, finally to start training with the Russian coaches in a traditional 2,000-seat Russian circus theater.

On arriving, we found a committee waiting to meet us outside the theater: the circus General Director and his staff. He happily explained that there were two shows the next day, full houses, "Nyet problema!" So I thanked him and shook his hand gratefully, honored to have them save seats for us to see the show. Before we gathered for a group news photo in front of the building, he proudly pointed to the marquee and with a curious sensation I recognized my name spelled in Russian. The General Director and Alla were beaming as the huge block letters in front of the theater were translated: "SOVIET-AMERICAN YOUTH CIRCUS, ROB MERMIN, DIRECTOR USA SOLD OUT!"

It turns out that you actually can feel your heart sink. As the implications slowly dawned, all I could do was gulp and try to remain standing, forcing myself to appear composed while the blood drained from my brain. That's when they took the picture.

I pulled Stewart aside and whispered that we were the show, matinee and evening, tomorrow, sold out! I had the curious satisfaction of watching the stunning realization cross Stewart's face. Both ashen-faced, we shook hands all around at the reception that followed, as if it were our last dinner on earth. It was an impossible predicament,

Soviet-American Youth Circus,
Yaroslavl, USSR

СОВЕТСКО-АМЕРИКАНСКИЙ ДЕТСКИЙ ЦИРК

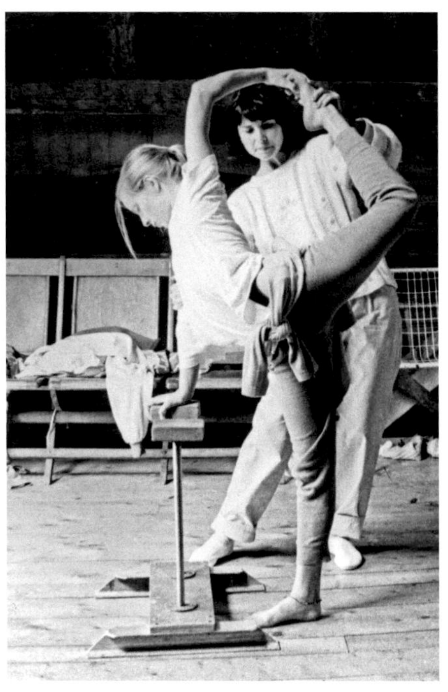

every performer's nightmare: waking up to a theater full of people waiting for the show to begin, and there you are on stage. Naked. In Soviet Russia.

What happened? The Soviet audiences in Yaroslavl, never having seen American circus performers, were enthusiastic. The troupers were marvelous, mixing acrobatic and juggling routines with the Russians and performing trapeze and wire and clowning with unfamiliar equipment, but with a grand sense of importance and gravity. For the two clowns, Robbo and Lippo, the two-hour shows were exercises in uninterrupted desperation and improvisation. We made nine entrances between the troupers' acts, in frenzied attempts to be funny for full houses of Soviets—despite frantic backstage antics looking for props and music tapes and bumping into each other every time we heard the spine-tingling cry, "CLOWNS!" Even now, I quiver in my clown shoes at the mere thought of Yaroslavl.

From Yaroslavl, the Soviet-American entourage traveled by train to Anapa, on the Black Sea. There they stayed at a Young Pioneer camp, where—as they practiced juggling and acrobatics on the beach—they became instant celebrities as the first Americans to visit.

They knew they were taking part in some sort of festival. They found themselves fighting a crowd to enter a massive, open-air soccer stadium. They were ushered into a gangway thronged with wildly costumed revelers, exotic animals, huge flags and shouting officials. Suddenly, over the loudspeaker, they heard, "Representing...the United States of America!" The parade moved, the U.S. national anthem burst out, the crowd roared, and unexpectedly they found themselves in front of a stadium full of 20,000 spectators and a parade of youth from several countries as part of the International Youth Festival on the Black Sea.

We all did double takes, looking at each other, wondering what to do. Swept up in a sudden fit of patriotic fervor I shouted, "March! Just march! And wave!" The troupers got into the swing of it, marching in formation around the track, waving and grinning madly, until they were compelled at the end to dash into the center of the field and perform wild acrobatic pyramids, with loud cowboy whoops and yelps and berserk yodeling under the tumultuous noise of the loudspeaker and the crowds. Jade Kindar-Martin put on stilts, others started tossing juggling clubs. It was all wonderfully strange, ending with a wild international mass dance to that year's musical hit song, "Lambada."

Still, to the annoyance of the American kids, the joint performances with the Russians mostly showcased the Russians' skills, and one night the Smirkus troupers' frustration spilled over in a tense meeting with Rob

"Watching them, it is difficult to say who is American, who is Russian. It is hard to say who gives more to the show: the professional Russian kids or the Americans, from their enthusiasm and desire to give themselves well.... It is like watching young flowers blossoming—they are the heart and soul of the future."

—Yuri Nikulen, beloved Russian clown and director of the Moscow Circus, upon seeing the first-ever demonstration of Soviet and American circus kids in the ring at the old Moscow Circus building

and Stewart. Stewart mildly suggested that, having seen how dedicated the Russian kids were, the Smirkus troupers might want to think about working on their skills year-round and not taking Smirkus for granted.

The Soviet excursion shifted Smirkus's course for good. It threw open the door to a fruitful collaboration with a series of coaches from what was soon to be the ex-Communist bloc, began a tradition of bringing young circus performers to Vermont from overseas and changed the company from an offbeat summer pastime to a premier circus proving ground. A small, idealistic group of young adults who wanted to find some way of passing on their deep love of circus was suddenly joining forces with people who quite sincerely considered circus their religion. "Circus is like a cathedral," Alla explains. "We are all like servants in a church for this art."

As it happened, Rob wasn't the only American who'd been in touch with Alla that year. Tim Holst, who spent two decades as Ringling's talent czar, was also interested in how The Greatest Show On Earth could make use of the incredible talent nurtured by the Soviet system. Alla had rebuffed Tim's offers of a job in the U.S. One day, he called her from China. "Alla, do you need anything?" he asked. "No, I'm fine," she responded, but then, seized with an idea, said, "Well, yes. I need eggs." Two days later, her doorbell rang. Tim was standing there with three flats of eggs. "Count them," he said. "I don't think I broke any. I held them on my lap all the way from Beijing." Pulled both by Tim's offer and by Rob—"Ten highly skilled coaches are less attractive than one person with that special charisma," she says—she agreed to tie up with Smirkus and go to work for Ringling as their director of new acts.

So when Alla led a group of young Russian circus performers and their parents to Greensboro a month after the Americans' visit, it was with a sense both of new possibility and of circus history being made. "Those two hoops that we were able to jump through—Russia and America—came together in history only once," says Alla. "They came together on that field in Greensboro. Before *perestroika*, it was ideologically impossible. Then history quickly changed again and it became commercially impossible. One very small window of history opened up for us, and we jumped in."

That first year the Russians came, we had huge problems getting them American visas. Two days before opening night I was prepared to do the tour without the Russians—and then suddenly the visas came through! We picked them up at the airport in New York, and decided that we'd use the visa problem as the opening of the show.

They'd all arrived with banged-up, old-style hard suitcases. So at showtime, I came out and announced, "Folks, I know we advertised this would be a Soviet-American circus, but we've had problems with visas and we'll just have to do the show without the Russians." So we'd start the opening act, then halfway through we'd be interrupted by a commotion from the aisles as the Russians came piling in from in front with their suitcases, shouting "Stop the show!" in Russian. I'd say, "The show just started, do you have your costumes?" They would point to their suitcases, go back and change and we were off! The Russians loved starting the show like that, it was right up their clown alley, poking fun at bureaucratic visa nonsense. There was cheering, and people actually wept when the Soviet and American kids came running out together for the first time. Remember, this was a time when the ice of the Cold War was just beginning to crack. The excitement of joint ventures in those days was electric.

Thus began our long Russian connection through the Circus Smirkus International branch office: Alla's living room in Moscow. For years, Alla arranged each summer to bring major Russian artists to Vermont, despite tremendous personal and bureaucratic difficulties securing documents during tenuous and often dangerous times. Meetings in Russia to arrange travel documents and sponsorships often resembled plots in a B-movie. Nefarious Russian officials and former KGB, dressed in dark suits and 1930s hats, arranged meetings with us in smoky offices, saunas, deserted warehouses and dimly lit nightclubs, to discuss dark diplomatic matters of cultural exchanges.

But we persevered. Throughout the 1990s, with great help from Charles Hosford of Project Harmony, Circus Smirkus hosted kids from Russia, Latvia, Ukraine, Mongolia, Kazakhstan, Hungary, Georgia, Siberia, Moldova, Canada, Japan, Indonesia, as well as from 10 Native American tribes and states all over the U.S. We became a truly international youth circus.

"Today was what peace is all about. Politics seem unreal and unnecessary when you join hands with a Russian performer to lift someone, when you help carry a Russian's equipment and have them stand on your shoulders. And when you hear in Russian but understand in English, that is when nothing else need exist but the people themselves and their words."

"Watching the Russians juggle really makes me want to spend the rest of my life in a room practicing. I've noticed that they will work and work on a trick until finally they get it. Then after accomplishing their goal, they continue to practice...forever. I have learned a tremendous lesson from them: Determination. Persistence. Overkill."

—Nolan Haims, trouper, diary excerpts from the Moscow trip

"I was shocked, then later impressed, when Rob called a council meeting with the American kids when they were in Russia. It really shook my system: here we only have meetings from the top down, called in a crisis, and we only listen. I thought anxiously, what is the crisis here? But the kids sat around and talked to Rob, the boss, so boldly, none of the Russians understood what was happening. Now I see it is just a natural expression of their feelings, and Rob not only accepted it, he asked for it!"

— Alla Youdina

Stewart Lippe's Russian Ripples

"Watching the Moscow Circus jugglers suggested to me that by simplifying these routines to the level of Circus Smirkus troupers I had a template for group juggling acts. I used this model to choreograph the group juggling acts for the next 10 years.

"The hard part was to teach aspiring teenage jugglers the intricacies of the patterns. Juggling demands repetition and there just was not enough time in the day to practice. So I instituted a 6:30 a.m. practice, in addition to the normal juggling rehearsal period. Once everyone was awake and out of bed we did a concentrated hour of juggling before breakfast, going over the choreography in a tent while the sun was coming up and the dew was still drying.

"And there was an incentive! If no clubs dropped on opening night, then I would buy them breakfast at the nearby Highland Lodge the next morning. This incentive lasted the whole tour. They thought I didn't want to spend money on a fancy breakfast—little did they know that the times I bought breakfast were the most satisfying money I've ever spent."

Trouper Contract

I, ____________________________, hereby accept the responsibilities and agree to learn the philosophy inherent in participation as a Circus Smirkus "Trouper." I vow to have FUN, learn something new every day, stretch my muscles and my imagination, and grow a little older, a little bolder this summer.

I UNDERSTAND that being a part of the Circus Family also involves a commitment to ensuring an environment where creativity and harmony can exist. One way this happens is to become aware of my behavior and interactions with others, in and out of the circus ring. The circus tent will be my Summer Home; I will look on the audience as invited guests to our living room, and welcome them with courtesy, for a time of entertainment and good company.

I REALIZE I WILL BE HELPING in various circus and household chores. This may include anything from sweeping, dishwashing and bathroom duty to backstage work with props, costumes, concessions and helping the tent crew. While on tour I agree to perform well not only in the ring, but with all backstage chores.

I WILL NOT BE ASHAMED of my mistakes in the ring. If I make a mistake, I'll make it grandly! I will learn to smile at my mistakes, with a determination to try again. Learning an act is only one part of my expectations: the traveling, circus work, meetings and making new friends is the total shared experience.

I WILL REMEMBER THAT I AM ESSENTIAL in creating the Smirkus image.

SOMETIMES I may have an "off" day when I make mistakes, do something stupid, act foolishly, am in a grumpy mood or simply feel exhausted. I will try not to give my bad moods to others. When I see it happening to someone else, I will understand it is his or her turn to be "off." I WILL TRY TO BE PATIENT AND KIND; I know my turn may come around. I will respect others' need for space and quiet when they need it and offer a listening ear or hug when appropriate.

Cartoon by Ed Koren

MY PROPS ARE MY PARTNERS; I will regard them as any friend requiring care, compassion and maintenance. I will respect the props of others.

I WILL BE FRIENDLY TO REPORTERS, answering questions thoughtfully and sincerely, while remembering I am the boss, not them: I can always politely but adamantly decline to answer any questions, personal or otherwise.

Smirkus is an ever-developing learning process for kids and adults. I KNOW RULES ARE NECESSARY while living closely in a group. Some rules may not always work the best, but I agree to try them first, as a code of behavior, and be open to working out reasonable alternatives, as needed, through group discussion at council meeting.

I understand Circus is A TIGHT-KNIT GROUP OF PEOPLE with various personalities and a multitude of idiosyncrasies. I will respect all kids and adults, regardless of age, sex, weight, color, religion, nationality, ability, etc.

I WILL ENDEAVOR TO WORK AS PARTNERS with the adults and try to understand their rights and needs, just as I expect them to recognize mine. I will listen to the coaches with respect for their experience and professionalism, even when I may not fully understand where their coaching is leading me.

Discipline in the group is really a matter of self-discipline. I WILL OFFER MY HELP as needed, and accept help when needing it, and abide by the decisions of the group at council meeting. I will accept the general rule that behavior disruptive to the group and inconsistent with this contract may result first in a verbal warning; second in a conference call with my parents/guardians; finally, in dismissal from the program.

I WILL SET MY OWN REALISTIC GOALS for the summer. Competition is with myself; cooperation is with others. I know there will always be some who are better than me at some things, others who are not as good. I will give when I can, and learn as I can.

Above all, in and out of the ring, I WILL LET MY OWN PERSONAL SPIRIT

S H I N E !

______________ ______________________________

date **trouper**

Guidelines for the Ring

(From Rob's Staff Memo Book)

One thing that sets Smirkus apart from other youth circus programs in America is that we are a circus. Other programs in the new "social circus" movement promote circus as recreation, circus as sport, circus as educational tool, circus as builder of self-esteem. These programs do a great job of promoting the social benefits circus bestows. But Smirkus promotes the centuries-old tradition of circus as a performing art and lifestyle. We see the social benefits as a by-product of what we do.

Smirkus has a distinct style and philosophy. It starts with one big thing: we come from the heart. The public knows what is fake and what is genuine; you can tell from the atmosphere in the tent and the tone of the applause how deeply the audience is affected. So we aim to work in the ring without pretension and out of the ring with generosity of spirit. We lift children up to higher standards of artistic aspiration while allowing them to be genuine to their own age and personality, and to let that spirit shine.

Guidelines for Troupers

- **When you miss a trick, recover with style and grace. No shaking of heads or frowns of frustration. For instance, jugglers: on first drop, pick up the prop quickly and continue without acknowledging a mistake. On second miss, react with grace and DON'T MAKE A BIG DEAL ABOUT IT. If you miss a third time and decide to try again, then acknowledge to the audience briefly that you "ain't given up yet." Build suspense and their encouragement using intention rather than ego. Then the third try becomes part of selling the act for all it's worth. Pause, take a breath, focus…. Then milk it!**
- **When you "style" or bow in acknowledgment to the audience: Look the audience directly in the eyes! Be present to them and not thinking mindlessly of what's for lunch. Be real, not smug, when taking a "style." Always acknowledge your partners. And acknowledge the whole audience, turning to all sides; don't ignore the "cheap" seats.**
- **When exiting, be waving at audiences in the seats near the curtain; do not relax your presence until well behind the curtain and past backstage.**
- **At no time should audience members be made to be embarrassed by a performer. Clowns should avoid vulgarity, ugliness, situations that would uncomfortably embarrass someone else or gratuitous violence out of context to traditional slapstick. This does NOT mean, heaven**

forbid, that we need to be "politically correct." Parody, satire, pure nonsensical slapstick, kicks in the butt, pants falling down, anarchy, rebellion, stupidity: clowns have license other humans lack! Check with the director.

- Every Smirkus show must at some time get the audience mildly wet. Why? The first Smirkus show turned the old confetti-in-a-bucket gag on its head. Twice. Creative variations on water-in-the-audience gags have lasted 25 years.
- Props and rigging are your partners. Treat them with fondness, care, respect and proper maintenance. Same with costumes. Be kind to them, if only as practice for being kind to people.
- The greatest misstep in this company is to show disrespect.

Guidelines for Staff

- Discourage mimicry of pop expectations in music, dress and attitude in the troupers. They need a respite from modern commercial culture, though they don't realize it until they get here and can breathe easier. They have unique personalities, they struggle with identity and they need freedom from outside influence.
- Discourage the misplaced competitive need to be "hip" and squash the "diva" clique. Discourage a star system in the ring. Encourage individuality, allow eccentricities, enjoy unique weirdness.
- Respect and nourish the ideals of youth. Idealism needs to flourish, even when jaded adult experience tells us it won't fly. We encourage dreams—indeed, the very existence of Smirkus is the evidence for promoting dreams. Recall your own youthful ideals; help them hold on to theirs.
- Don't accept backtalk. Demand they look you in the eyes, head up, when talking to you. Give respect; require it in return.
- Don't overdo praise. Excessive praise unwittingly sets up cockiness.

The tent is our summer home. The ring is a space with a history and tradition that must be respected, and which gives that space a certain sacredness. Creation happens there; magic surrounds the audience there. The air in that space has tension and elasticity. Feel it, absorb it, respect it and, above all, protect it.

Finally, be proud to work "under canvas," the old term for going out with a tent show, through whatever the elements throw your way: rain, mud, heat, thunder and lightning. Later in life you will have stories for the grandkids and a clear sense of having paid your dues in this business. Be content to look with mild, half-concealed condescension at those in the business who have never played under canvas.

Remembering...

Marcel Marceau

(1923-2007)

By Rob Mermin

I began the study of mime in 1969 in Paris, at the invitation of the master himself for the inaugural class at L'Ecole Internationale de Mime Marcel Marceau.

Above: Marcel Marceau in the ring with the Smirkus troupers. **Left:** Marceau in the ring. **Below:** Marceau with Rob Mermin as Robin Hood.

I also studied with Marceau's mentor, Étienne Decroux, who was still teaching in his tiny Parisian basement studio. The world of a mime is in the theater, giving expression to artistic vision. The world of a circus artist is in the ring, displaying physical achievement mixed with a lifestyle between sawdust and canvas. The blend of the two worlds encompasses centuries of overlapping traditions.

Marceau loved the circus but had never performed in a circus ring. In 1999 he agreed to perform a benefit show under the Circus Smirkus big top in Middlebury, Vermont. We had rented a large fancy trailer for his dressing room parked behind the tent. He sat in it looking doubtful. Outside he could hear the shouts and laughter of the circus troupers preparing for the show. When I nervously checked in before the show I found him edgy. I had suggested earlier that he perform his comical "Tightrope Walker" act, but he was appalled: "Non!" he cried, pacing. "How can my invisible tightrope walker compete with the real thing?"

The maestro was already anxious about the soft ring carpet and the technical limitations of the tent. I warned his technical director not to push the lights to their full brightness, as Marceau liked, because this would blow out our system. As the show began, the sold-out crowd was electric, the tent buzzing with anticipation. When Marceau began his first number I glanced nervously at the lights. They were definitely up way too high. Sure enough, barely 30 seconds later the lights blew and the tent plunged into silent blackout. My heart stopped. Then in the sudden darkness we heard impressive cursing in French. I ran out to escort the maestro backstage, bumping into him in the blackness.

After what seemed like years of backstage panic, the lights miraculously came on and Marceau commenced from the top. It took all his virtuosity and several acts before he relaxed into what was for him the awkwardness of the ring. It was a revelation to see him carefully adjust his performance to accommodate a full audience in the round.

Sometimes calamity is prelude to an experience of profound grace. By the finale Marceau was beaming in a way I had never seen, as the audience rose as one in standing ovation. The magic of the big top had engulfed him. Marceau raised his hand to quiet the cheering audience and began to speak in his soft, wispy voice. The astonished crowd hushed. Never before in his 50-year career had he spoken, in costume, in front of an audience.

Marceau, deeply moved, gathered the troupers all around him in the ring. He spoke for 15 minutes of the power of art for bringing people together and the power of silence for bridging generations. The warmth and love in the tent were palpable. People saw three generations of mentors standing in the ring together: Marceau and myself; me with Jade and Molly; and all the Smirkos these two ex-troupers had affected that summer. Moist eyes filled the tent that night.

Marceau loved the circus, with its grace and beauty, comedy and drama, and its metaphors for the human struggle to achieve despite the obstacles in life. He lyrically wrote: "The circus is loved in the whole world. Like music, it explains nothing. Rather, it touches your heart by the risks circus artists take, not only through physical movements, but by the poetry they give with their soul." We are honored to have given him the only experience of his career under a Big Top.

"The circus is loved in the whole world.
Like music, it explains nothing.
Rather, it touches your heart
by the risks circus artists take,
not only through physical movements,
but by the poetry they give
with their soul."

CHAPTER FIVE

DREAMS of ADVENTURE

Spreading Whimsy, Conjuring Delight, Evoking Wonder

We loved, loved, loved coaching at Smirkus. It teaches the fundaments of what circus really is—the charm and beauty and passion you have to have to be a circus performer. You're not just learning a circus skill, not just learning to do a somersault, but learning to be a performer from the heart.

—Tosca Zoppé, seventh-generation member of the Zoppé Family Circus

"In the years since I left Smirkus, I've lived scenes in my professional career that harken back to it. At the world circus festival in Moscow, I was the last performer leaving. This little old technician comes running up and grabs me and takes me down the halls and tunnels of the Moscow Circus, and finally we come to this room and it's all the Russian technicians—these were people who'd been performers in the '40s and '50s—with vodka and pickles. They'd seen some Russian connection in my wire act: they appreciated the technique—the basic technique came from Smirkus coach Nina Malachikhina—and the way of presenting the number really touched them. They singled me out as someone they recognized. I'll never be able to pin down why my act works so well with Russians, but it does, and I think it comes directly from what we learned at Smirkus with those Russian coaches."

—Molly Saudek, medal winner at circus festivals in Moscow, Paris, Budapest

One day during training in Greensboro, four visiting Russian coaches approached Barb Baird and mimed that they wanted her to take them fishing. She agreed, the men climbed into the back of her pickup truck, and they headed to a local lake.

Taking a shortcut down a logging road, the truck got stuck in the mud. Whatever Barb tried, the wheels spun helplessly. Exasperated, she sat in the cab trying to figure out what to do. The four men fanned out, squatted and, with Barb still in it, lifted the truck out of the ooze and carried it to solid ground. "That," she says, "is when I realized Smirkus was in a completely different world with them."

The advent of the Russians, as Rob had expected, changed Smirkus forever.

Through the pipeline he'd opened with Alla spilled an array of talented coaches and young performers who, for a few magic months each summer, plugged the barn into the international circus community. They brought with them not just muscles hardened through long years of relentless training, but a dedication to the artistry of circus, an attachment to discipline and a seriousness of purpose that were at first an odd match for the more exuberant, happy-go-lucky Smirkus style.

Alla served as a conduit for Smirkus to both Russia and Ringling, and still managed, as head coach, to teach trapeze, cloud swing, bungee, rings and acrobatics and to create innovative new acts for over a decade. She brought over Volodya Avgustov and his wife, Zina, along with Gennady Totukhov—they taught acrobatics, hand balance and the perch pole that would become a staple of Smirkus shows—and convinced Chimgee Haltarhuu, a Mongolian contortionist and acrobat, that Greensboro was the perfect spot for her young son Tamir to spend his summers. They were joined for a season or two by world-renowned Russian coaches. Alla and her colleagues, highly trained artists all, found something deeply satisfying in the Vermont woods. "I believe something magical happens here in this environment," she once said. "An atmosphere full of charm and genuine feeling is created. Maybe it is because we are working like the Russian traveling circus of 100 years ago, in a small tent, with the smell of hay spread out on the grass for children to sit on."

Smirkus was an exhilarating place before the advent of the Russians, but as a circus its emphasis had been on the joys of performing rather than on exploring the heights to which athleticism and technical ambition could take its troupers. Now those considerations came into balance. The troupers began to see that what had been a quirky summer pastime also let them say something serious about their place in the world. "I remember a conversation with Alla," says Molly Saudek. "She was describing circus as this battle between mankind and the elements, and its resolution. We take things human beings are not supposed to be able to do—fly, work with fire, communicate with animals, manipulate our world in impossible ways—and in doing so we find a deeper communication with the world."

As the visiting troupers and the American kids performed side by side for cheering audiences, played stickball in the field and worked with each other to master complicated pyramids and dervish-like chains of back handsprings, they taught one another. "The Russian teens learned a lot from us about the way an audience will respond to you as a person doing these amazing things," recalls Porter Lontz-Underhill, a regular trouper in the early 1990s. "They learned how to let their love of what they were doing show. And what we learned from the Russian kids was that there was a level of professionalism and polish and skill that we could aspire to, not as adults, but right now, as a 14-year-old kid. Ultimately that's the thing that got people working out in their backyards at home during the school year, whether it was walking on a wire or doing pushups, was meeting the Russians and understanding the level of dedication it takes.

An equally fertile cultural exchange was taking place among the adults. Partners Julie Greenberg and Jeff Jenkins arrived at Smirkus in 1995 from Chicago as coaches, and would spend hours training with the Russian coaches, learning technique—and suffering just as much as the troupers did. "There really wasn't any other place in the U.S. that you could train under such accomplished artists," says Jeff.

But Jeff, Julie, Rob and the other Americans were also teaching the Russians. "We understood how to tell a story using skills, rather than just presenting skills, and they responded to that," Julie remembers. "We could add a comedic twist, help them build a connection to the audience. They learned from us how to reach an American audience."

In the winter, with Alla, Rob, Zina, Volodya, Chimgee, Tamir—and, for a time, eventual director Troy Wunderle and his wife, Sara—living at the Barn, Smirkus headquarters became a tiny year-round circus village. Between their comings and goings for Ringling or other circuses, they would plan the next season and dream up acts for the following year. Volodya created props and rigging with found materials around the barn, including old farm equipment, using pipe, rope and pulleys from old tractors to make inspiration real.

This encounter between eastern discipline and western showmanship produced what troupers who were there at the time still think of as a Smirkus "golden era," a focused cross-cultural community of coaches and experienced troupers who united to fashion the unique Smirkus blend of spirited storytelling, technical ambition, artistic inventiveness and sunny exuberance. The result, Julie says, was that the Barn "became this place where we could create together these shows that were beautiful and poignant and inspiring. And then we would take all these ideas we'd tried out on the kids and take them back to our professional lives."

"Rob had a special ability to create an open environment for us all to work," says Alla. "He'd bring children to the point where they had no strings holding them back: the strings of parents or the strings of rules. They were like birds released from cages—so happy to fly. We wouldn't tell them, *'Don't, don't, don't*—don't climb, don't scream, don't run, don't jump.' It was the opposite: *Do* run, *do* climb, *do* jump, *do* scream. The adults, the coaches and counselors, shared the same excitement, so we created together."

This collaboration with Alla was an always-fascinating experiment in cross-cultural creativity. Besides working on new acts, our nightly discussions about art, culture and history were inspirational. I witnessed her professional and personal charm have its effect on the troupe. She assessed children professionally, and could see what a child might accomplish well before anyone else.

On the American side, Stewart's eye as a technical director for lighting and staging was as important as his sideshow skills. Even more valuable, he had a natural talent for bonding with the troupers, and his underlying sense of history and steadfast humor helped establish the Smirkus mentality.

Jeff Jenkins was a master in the world of American slapstick and physical comedy. He received instant respect from troupers simply by standing there.

As the creative ferment of the 1990s took hold, Smirkus began making a name for itself in the circus community. Not only did its shows command attention from the pros, it began producing a series of talented performers who made their way into the world at large. Jade Kindar-Martin became an internationally known high-wire virtuoso who earned two Guinness world records, first for the longest duo wire walk, across the Thames

"I was drawn to the foreign Smirkos like a magnet—I had a big mouth and was not about to exclude them from my antics just because we couldn't speak to one another. There was an energetic Russian boy named Anton. Being young teenagers we thought it was wise to teach one another curse words in our native tongues. We were given a stern warning. Not willing to break the international code of boyhood, I proceeded to reveal the foulest words in my vocabulary anyway: pillowcase, handkerchief and Kuchler—since Adam Kuchler was there for my teachings. Every word I said made Adam laugh, which made Anton think it was a really bad word. I knew this ploy had succeeded when, weeks into the tour, I overheard a trouper say, 'Why does Anton walk by me, say "pillowcase" and laugh?'"

—Sam Johnson,
former trouper

"You'd never see the Russian coaches training. So you'd think their demands were ridiculous. Then Vladimir would put his wife upside-down on his head and do what he'd just asked you to do, and you'd think 'Oh, OK. I guess I should be able to do that.'"

—Dan Brown,
former trouper

River in London in 1997, and again in 2007 for the longest wire-walk on record, a one-kilometer race across the Han River in Seoul, South Korea. Molly Saudek went on to win medals at international circus competitions and thrilled audiences with her vivacious wire dance for Cirque Eloize, the Big Apple Circus, Cirque du Soleil and European circuses. Molly Pelley and Adam Kuchler established what became an ongoing clown pipeline between Smirkus and Ringling Bros. and Barnum & Bailey. Cris Clark toured with Ringling as an aerialist and became an all-around circus renaissance man—including for Smirkus, where he has been a coach and head rigger. Sam Johnson created his own troupe—The Big Aerial Show—for state fairs across the country. Kaleen McKeeman originated the title role for Cirque Du Soleil's *Zaia*; she then joined a parade of later Smirkos, including Mason Ames, Eric Bates and Jacob Stein-Sharpe, as part of the up-and-coming Montreal troupe Les Sept

Doigts de la Main. The list of dozens of star professionals coming out of this little circus in the woods is entirely out of proportion to its size.

The mix of demanding coaches and troupers who returned year after year also produced a new spirit—a belief that Smirkus was not just a summer diversion, but a year-round avocation. When the Russian pipeline began to dry up because of visa issues in the late 1990s, says Ozzie, "our kids stood up and said, 'Hey, now it's our turn!' You don't get that kind of energy out of something you've had to do all your life; you get that energy out of something you *want* to do, and they were raring to go." Kids would leave at the end of a tour and train all fall, winter and spring—on a wire strung between trees in their backyard, with juggling balls down in the basement, hanging from a bar in a barely heated neighbor's barn or in one of the new circus training facilities that were cropping up around the country.

For American kids, this was mostly fun; they wanted to have a fun time. But they had not learned how to work hard yet. If I pushed hard, they complained, "I'm tired, it's a hot day, can I take a break?" In Mongolia, until our teacher says, "You're dismissed!" you don't say anything. And in my culture you're not going to hear, "Great!" My first year at Circus Smirkus, I don't think I ever said, "Good job." The kids would ask, "Why does Chimgee never say how I'm doing?" I'd say, "OK, you're working hard, we need to work more." The kids had heard all the time from American coaches, "Good job! Good job!" but I was like, "It wasn't a good job. Not yet."

—Chimgee Haltarhuu,
longtime Smirkus aerial and acrobatic coach

The years 1998 and 1999—the *Rock 'n Roll Show* and *Robin Hood*—were pivotal, a time for Smirkus to stretch its wings. The new Italian-made big top allowed for the most complex rigging Smirkus had yet produced, including in 1998 a seven-lane cradle hung with ropes that showcased most of the troupe in the air. In 1999, Smirkus not only produced a scripted show with dialogue, but used horses in the ring, rigged a tightwire 15 feet in the air, commissioned an original music score and showcased legendary circus equestrian Alberto Zoppé in the ring. Marcel Marceau performed in the tent. Disney filmed a 15-part documentary Smirkus television series. The old farm was alive with creativity.

The bareback horse act, coached by Alberto and his daughter Tosca, was a sterling example of what Smirkus was capable of—teaching nonequestrians not just to stand on moving horses, but to build three-high pyramids on them in a mere three weeks. "They sat us down and said, 'You need to remember this is going to require all day every day of training,'" recalls Francey Grund, who was part of that act. "But the opportunity to learn from a seventh-generation circus family a skill that I knew in the real world would take *months* to accomplish was the ultimate expression of what Smirkus is—that as a group of

"Smirkus inspired a passion for excellence, the humanity required to share of one's self, and the courage to try."

—Jay Mireault, father of acrobat and juggler Al Mireault

KGB Busted in Hardwick

"A new Russian delegation was coming to Vermont after the successful first cultural exchange. Alla again needed a Russian sponsor to pay for the venture. It turned out to be a major transport company that saw Smirkus as a possible cover operation—an innocent nonprofit children's charity—for making inroads into the U.S.

So along with the Russian circus kids and coaches, we got a boss from the Russian sponsor and two suspicious-looking officials who were supposedly from Soyuzgostsirk. They turned out to be KGB. As long as they stayed out of the way, I had no time for politicking—I had a show to mount.

One o'clock in the morning, rehearsal period. The Russians have been here for two weeks. Exhausted from a long day, I awake to a knock on my door. It's the Hardwick Village police. They want to know what to do with two drunken Russians who don't speak English and keep mumbling "Seer-kus Shmeer-kus." I go down to the police station and there are the two KGB, handcuffed to a radiator. I smile. Apparently they'd stolen my car, driven across some fields and ended up in a haystack.

"OK," I tell the officers. "You've locked up the Soviet KGB! Play along with me, I'll act outraged and we'll keep them handcuffed for a while. Let's give them a show." So for 45 minutes I yelled at the cops, sometimes pleading, then shouting and gesticulating madly, pointing back and forth to the worried prisoners. The officers threatened to take out their pistols. Finally, we shared some doughnuts with the prisoners and I took out my wallet. With my back to the prisoners, I pretended to bribe the officers, who then smiled and uncuffed the Russians. I nodded to them and said, in Russian, "Let's go. Everything OK." Suddenly I was a big shot with the KGB.

The upshot of this story is history: the KGB guys returned to Russia, no doubt embellished this story about their terrifying ordeal inside the hostile American penal system, which of course struck fear into the hearts of the KGB bureaucracy, which then caused panic in the Kremlin and six months later the Soviet Union collapsed. The Smirkus influence indeed reaches far...." —Rob Mermin

teenagers we shouldn't be able to put together a bareback act in three weeks, but we did."

In 2000, after a couple of years off, Jeff and Julie returned from Chicago, bringing with them a new Mongolian coach, Bat, and a new set of artistic and stylistic elements. They introduced choreography, disciplines like Russian Bar and teeterboard, and a push to make the closing act—which came to be known as *voltige*—more pyrotechnic. These acts were highly choreographed and vigorously acrobatic, involving teeterboard and other ways of making people fly through the air. "They demanded a sense of focus and intensity that made

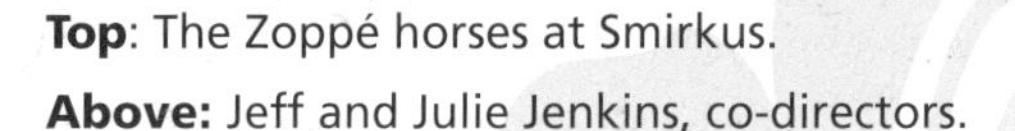

Top: The Zoppé horses at Smirkus.
Above: Jeff and Julie Jenkins, co-directors.

them feel like a very professional act," says Tristan Cunningham, a trouper from that era. "If you were part of it, you were learning to be a professional."

For a pair of urban performers, Jeff and Julie were taken with what Rob and Smirkus had carved out of the Vermont fields. In 1995, Julie remembers, Jeff, a former Ringling clown and now a slapstick master coach, came home one day in the middle of winter from Ringling Clown College auditions and said, "I just met this man, Rob Mermin, he wants me to take his show on tour because he's become director of the Clown College and he can't do it."

Jeff: *So this magical, mysterious, quirky, visionary clown steps aside and a couple of young, brash city folk from Chicago swoop in and try to steer this thing around Vermont. . . It was an adventure I will never forget. It was a wild assortment of fearless kids and a colorful (to put it mildly) tent crew and staff and Russians all thrown together. It was intense and creative, not just from an artistic standpoint, but from a day-to-day, let's-keep-it-moving, get-the-tent-up-do-a-show-and-get-the-heck-out-of-town sort of way!*

Julie: *It was culture shock! We were city folk, and it was sooooo homegrown. We were completely out of touch and out of our element. At first it seemed like the troupers knew more about what was going on than the grownups did. I was thinking, "These are kids? Because they're acting like adults, and they seem more responsible than most adults I know, but they still know how to play, which makes them cooler than most adults we know." But I quickly knew this was a place that would change my life. It was a whole different way of working than I'd been used to. The work was not just work. It was a lifestyle: it was about community. And because the kids were willing and said "Yes," and because Rob gave us a platform to do it, the shows began to change.*

Jeff: *The Russians raised the bar acrobatically, and Smirkus started to grow and audition kids outside of the rural Vermont region. Circus itself was growing and gaining a bigger audience: Big Apple Circus, Cirque du Soleil, Eloize, Midnight Circus, we were all doing new things in the circus world and the kids who would become troupers were witnessing this and wanted to be part of it.*

In 2002, the ground once again shifted under Smirkus's feet. Rob had written and directed that year's show, *Legends of the Wild West.* For the first time since the early days, it had a live band, the Route 7 Ramblers, a bluegrass quartet from Middlebury College. The clown trio of Ryan Combs, Sam Brown and John Stokvis, who'd been working together since 1999, had become a force to be reckoned with; that year they created a water-spitting cowboy shootout that, a decade later, is still considered one of the high points of Smirkus clowning.

But that summer Rob had to deal with a serious cancer diagnosis. Too ill for touring, he turned over the tour to Troy Wunderle to take his part in the ring with the troupers. He had already recruited Indian hoop dancers and trick ropers from the Southwest. "In the Smirkus ring I had played a pirate captain, a rock 'n roll star, an astronaut and Robin Hood," Rob says. "I was frustrated not getting to play a cowboy!"

Jeff and Julie went on to direct the next two seasons, bringing a new flavor to the

Old Blue

"I designed the first Smirkus tent with a blue top, green walls and yellow valance to represent the blue skies, green mountains and summer sun of Vermont. We managed to stuff 500 people in there. The mystical signage over the ring—the painted sun, moon and earth faces staring out to the audience—were designs taken from a centuries-old tarot deck. The earth's eyes, Mona Lisa-style, follow you wherever you move inside the tent.

As the years went by, holes began appearing in the top. Every winter, alone at the barn, I would drag the heavy bags containing the three top sections up to the second-floor studio and spread out a section at a time. Each section covered the whole barn floor. I would be on my knees for hours cutting vinyl stars with extra tent fabric, and with glue and heat gun apply them over every little pinhole. Each summer when the tent was raised everyone counted the new stars that appeared inside the tent against the dark blue top as if by magic over the winter. After 10 years the tent was proudly sprinkled with night-sky constellations.

By 1998, Old Blue had weathered storms, mud slides, even a small tornado; that year, for the first time, it was set up on the hill behind the sheds, relegated to being a practice tent. For Smirkus had bought a brand new big top from Italy, a four-mast, 80-foot round-top with new bleachers, seating 750. The new tent, called the Chapiteau, was raised on the main field for the new show.

When it was finished the whole company—staff, troupers, coaches, everyone—ran excitedly down to the Chapiteau and gathered inside to celebrate. I was standing on the porch of the farmhouse with Julie watching the mass exodus to the new tent. Then I looked in the other direction at Old Blue in the distance, alone upon the hill, forlorn as an empty tent can be. Abandoned after a decade of loyal service! Julie got wet eyes. Later that evening at council I told the story of Old Forgotten Blue and the troupe got very quiet. Then the troupers suggested a Gratitude Ceremony to be held in Old Blue, a celebration of her service and fame. We held the next council up on the hill inside Old Blue and told tour stories, looked at her stars and the new holes marking her weathered skin, and gloried in her atmosphere. Old Blue went on to be the clowning tent at Smirkus Camp, with eager beginning circus campers looking up at her stars and dreaming of becoming a Smirkus trouper. After many years of service and fine old age, she is now retired, resting quietly in the barn." —Rob Mermin

Chapiteau: faster-paced, more urban, more electric, more knowing. They brought in costume designers to give the troupers a new sheen in the ring for 2003's superhero show, *Smirkopolis: The Legion of Laughter*, and in 2004 hired composer Peter Bufano and his Cirkestra to write and perform the score for *Smirkus Through the Looking Glass*, giving Smirkus an altogether louder and more worldly sound.

The shows they directed were polished and technically daring, flaunting the skills of a generation of Smirkus aerialists and acrobats whose year-round training allowed them to bring the tent to a new pitch of excitement. "As Smirkus grew," says Jeff, "so did audience expectations. We felt that it was important to present a show that met those expectations: great acrobatics, professional costumes, clean, focused and funny clowning, all without losing the heart of Smirkus."

Jeff and Julie's directing style was different from Rob's, but in the same way that Rob paid close attention to kids' personalities and how they could bring out their character, Jeff and Julie designed acts to show off their raw material. "They were really experts at allowing you to bring forward your energy and personality, and then they would shape and guide that into something that would fit in the overall structure, yet allow you to really shine," says Abby Suskin, a trouper from 2000 to 2005.

In 2006, Smirkus's direction changed again when it hired Troy Wunderle and Jesse Dryden to co-direct. The two had met as Rob and Jeff's students a decade before, the year Rob had co-directed Ringling's Clown College. After a season touring with Ringling, Troy joined Smirkus in 1997, helping Rob do residencies in schools during the off-season and serving as all-around assistant in the summer at the camp and tour.

Jesse, for his part, had spent seven years coaching at Smirkus Camp—eventually becoming head coach—and working with Troy on school residencies during the year. Eventually, he left to work for Cirque du Soleil, which is where he was when the possibility of directing Smirkus opened up.

While Troy and Jesse's working style is closer to Jeff and Julie's than to Rob's—they, too, arrive at training in June with a clear idea of the show they intend to mount, the acts it will contain and how they'd like to cast the troupers who will populate those acts—their joint sensibility is a mix of the two. Troy was always a louder, broader, more hammy clown than Rob's nuanced, mime-inspired version, but he essentially grew up in the circus world as Rob's protégé. He considers it his role to protect Smirkus's in-the-ring innocence. Jesse, who lives year-round in Montreal, one of the world's capitals of new circus, is altogether more theatrical and willing to take risks. The two ought not to be able to work together—and yet the 2012 show will be their seventh together.

An interview with co-directors Troy Wunderle and Jesse Dryden

So how do you divide responsibilities?

JESSE: The way I've taken to describing it is, I'm NASA and he's Mission Control. I come up with the project, design it and help launch it. Then Troy keeps it in orbit and fixes it as it goes along, and eventually brings it home safely.

TROY: I give Jesse as much support and freedom as possible during training, because I have the next seven or eight weeks to perfect the show while we're out on the road. There isn't a single day all summer when I'm not rewriting.

What do you look for when you're auditioning troupers?

JESSE: My cold-hearted argument, speaking purely as a professional, is that the very nature of auditioning is putting yourself up for rejection. If you haven't prepared yourself for that—or if you're a parent and haven't prepared your child for it—you shouldn't go through this process. The show is the solid ground

I can stand on: I've got the show in my head and they just don't fit. It's a harsh process, because who knows how much talent has slipped under our noses.

TROY: I sometimes get criticized for not always selecting the best talent outright. But talent only matters to me if it's accompanied by a kind heart and passionate personality. I need to believe kids will not only survive the day-to-day challenges, but thrive throughout the entire experience. They need to understand that this experience is a gift and that the group is more important than the individual. These factors are just as important to me as whether or not they're the world's best juggler, the most graceful aerialist or the funniest clown. Casting kids with great skill, exuberant smiles, humble hearts and joyful personalities continues to be our recipe for success.

You guys do things differently from the way Rob did. He liked to watch what kids were doing in training and build from there. But now, even before they arrive you've got an idea of what you want them to do.

JESSE: Rob loved the whole idea of letting everyone discover everything; he loved the exploration and play. But I feel the pressure of being asked, in three weeks, to produce a marketable and ticket-worthy product. Don't get the wrong idea, though—you also have to listen to the show. You have to say the show is pointed in this direction, but it's a lot like sailing: you've got to let the wind blow you around a bit, so you can discover the secret talents or directions a kid might head.

TROY: We don't cast the entire show by simply considering who is technically and physically best in each role. If we were to cast only by talent, there would be some kids in several acts and others in none. That would not make for a great environment, a great cast or a great show.

JESSE: The clowns are a good example. We cast "clown clowns" and "rigging clowns," and we pair them up so that junior clowns can learn from senior clowns, which means that returning clowns don't always get the biggest parts. The idea is always to pair a strong returning clown with new clowns, so that they're learning from each other.

TROY: We warn troupers not to expect a solo act simply because they've grown up with us. Our troupe benefits greatly from casting senior troupers as key members of group acts. Owen Winship demonstrated this during the 2011 *Frontpage Follies* show. He could easily have carried a solo rola bola act, but instead paired himself with younger troupers to create unique circus magic within our ring. He and his fellow performers showcased the power of trusting one another wholeheartedly.

And then, of course, things change during training...

TROY: A week and a half in, we're already looking at coaches and saying, "This act's not going to make it." And sometimes we see that a trouper's body won't be able to handle the strain of what we'd planned. It's our job to mentor them on how to care for their bodies long-term.

One of the things I've noticed about Smirkus shows is that the directors pay a lot of attention to timing, pacing, the emotional atmosphere in the tent. There must be details to this that the audience doesn't even notice.

JESSE: Take transitions between acts. The transitions are what make the show move. We don't fade to black, we don't try to misdirect the audience's attention. We say, "Hey! Look at this rigging! Isn't it cool?" I've noticed theatrically that it helps to build up the tension. You never want the audience to feel they can leave their seats. You want them not to know what the next emotion is going to be. You want to slow them down, control their breath almost, so they're gasping at the right moment and then laughing the next moment. That's where circus thrives.

Troy, you and Rob are very different performers—he's more understated and European and you're louder and more Ringling—yet there seems to be a lot of him in your approach toward Smirkus.

TROY: We share a touch of silly and a sense of comedic wonder. We both believe in professionalism, humility, sincerity, optimism and the innocence of youth. We try to improve the world around us by using Smirkus as a voice to showcase a better way. We are passionate about finding a way to live and succeed as a commune of artists with the united goal of spreading joy. So I often feel like I am a referee between Rob's vision of what Smirkus should be and Jesse and the creative team's ideas of what Smirkus could become. Jesse makes sure their creative juices keep flowing. I'm in charge of holding emotions in check and making sure that our final product is full of Smirkus flavor.

Hole in the Wall

When Rob worked with Cirkus Benneweis in Copenhagen in the early '70s, once a year the circus opened its doors to children from around the country with severe disabilities and life-threatening illnesses. It took two days for them to converge on the circus building, traveling by bus, train and ship. When they finally arrived, the building was filled with 2,000 children in various stages of illness, some excitedly jabbering with their friends, others quiet, withdrawn, in wheelchairs, shaking uncontrollably, but all of them staring at the ring. Rob found himself wondering, "Can I really run out there and do backflips, shake hands and act silly in front of these kids?" He could, and found the day one of the most stirring of his career. Each year at Benneweis, all the artists looked forward to this powerful event, agreeing it was the best audience ever.

So Rob made a habit of it as he worked his way through dozens of countries: he would seek out an orphanage or children's hospital to visit with his bag of tricks. He worked for no charitable organization; it was just a personal, unauthorized visit. "As usual," he says, "some grownups complained about the lack of official process. The kids never complained."

Having seen what a circus performance could do for children in need, Rob—along with Ozzie—made sure that Smirkus carried on the tradition. This was never more true than in 1999 and for a few years afterward: on a travel day in the middle of the tour, Ozzie would drive the troupe down to perform for the kids at Paul Newman's Hole in the Wall Gang Camp in northeastern Connecticut. The camp, which opened a year after Smirkus got its start, gives kids with terminal and life-threatening illnesses—cancer, sickle-cell anemia, HIV/AIDS and the like—a chance to swim, camp, boat, ride horses, do crafts and art projects and all the other things that other children get to take for granted in the summer. It does all this completely free of charge.

For many troupers, this was an unexpectedly profound, and even humbling, moment. Standing behind the curtain waiting to go on, Kerren McKeeman unconsciously echoed Rob's thoughts years before. "Most spectators are immediately inspired by our teamwork, physical ability and energy," she later wrote in an essay about the show. "Yet how can I possibly inspire these children whose lives and experiences are limited by their physical conditions? How can I perform handstands and acrobatics for children in wheelchairs?"

Members of the audience were hooked up to life-support machines, they were frail, balding from chemotherapy, sometimes unable to stand, and the troupers keenly felt the difference between the two sides of the performing-arts center. But once onstage, their jitters disappeared. "To my absolute delight," Kerren wrote, "the children cheer more enthusiastically throughout this show than any audience I have ever seen. Those who can, rise out of their chairs, clapping and yelling, their faces radiating complete joy. After the performance some children greet us on stage with personally crafted thank-you cards and orange Hole in the Wall Gang Camp key chains."

The troupers were not just moved; in some cases, they were transformed. They had arrived expecting to inspire other kids. Instead, they found themselves inspired by the courage and enthusiasm that surrounded them.

"We knew that some of them didn't have much longer to live," recalls Dan Brown. "So when they gave us a standing ovation at the end of our show, that was hands down the most memorable moment of my life. It wasn't just knowing that we were able to bring them a slice of happiness. This experience trivialized everything else in our lives—every bickering moment, every beef you had with someone for not washing pots. I carry that with me more than anything else from Smirkus—it was the hardest thing I had to do, and the best thing." For her part, Kerren carried with her that orange key chain, with all her keys on it, until well after college.

Smirko Moments

A PIE IN THE FACE

It was the juggling act of 1994, a café scene with Doug Bair as the maître d' and Chris Grabher as the hapless customer. Waiters, chefs, plates, food and "wine bottles" were flying everywhere. At the end, Doug would bring out an enormous bill, walking around slowly showing it to the entire audience before giving it to Chris. This time, Doug had prepared a pie and hid it with the bill and a sign that read, "Free Dessert." Everyone in the audience saw it first, and everyone knew what Chris was about to get—except Chris. It was the most nonchalant, perfectly executed pie buildup in a quarter-century of pies.

WATER COUNCIL

Every summer, there must be one gathering at which the troupers, unsuspecting, get mercilessly doused. The year Rob was unable to go on tour because of his illness, the company pulled into Simsbury, Connecticut, and set up behind a fire station. In between shows, Troy called the troupe together to announce that Rob seemed to be doing better, and he thought a get-well cast photo was called for. He positioned everyone outside the tent, with their backs to the fire station—and to the fire truck parked innocently beside it. At a pre-arranged signal from Troy, a geyser of water arced into the air... and fell about 40 yards short. But Troy had had the foresight to get the kids chanting "Smirko!" and the din was so loud no one heard the misfire. The next shot landed right on target, scattering kids in every direction.

WEIGH-STATION ETIQUETTE

It was 2004. Driving along the highway, the bus with all the troupers pulled into a weigh station to get inspected. Because it was carrying all the troupers' suitcases plus a large pile of four-foot iron tent stakes, it exceeded its legal weight limit. The tent crew had pulled in behind, so the troupers piled out, formed a stake brigade, and started shifting the heavy stakes from the bus onto a different truck. The weigh-station attendant, moved by the sight of so many kids working happily to get the job done, threw bureaucracy to the winds. "Never mind!" he told them, and waved them on.

A STOIC COMIC MOMENT

In a 1996 act for *Lights, Action, Circus!*, character clown Richard Saudek comes out snarfing down a bag of popcorn while wooing a young lady from the audience. Unknown to him, one day hot chili powder was sprinkled over the popcorn. Brave little Richard stole the show as usual and made it through the whole bag without a visible sign of distress, then fairly exploded, bug-eyed, out the back door.

A STOIC MOMENT
THAT WASN'T MEANT TO BE COMIC

The 2011 *Frontpage Follies* tour was plagued by boys' pants that didn't always have the give to accommodate the stretching demanded by a circus performance. This was revealed to the troupe and a tentful of audience members by Nick Zelle, who at the beginning of a dramatic rope act climbed to the top of the tent and went into a legs-akimbo split...only to rip the crotch of his pants from front to back. There was nothing to do—he performed the entire act with his customary flair, finished up, styled grandly and left the spotlight... only to have to come back into the ring immediately for the finale, without having had a chance to get his pants sewn up.

FUN CELEBRITY MOMENT I

Chef Julia Child came to the show in the early

'90s. Nervously, the Smirkus cooks served her lunch from the pie car: chicken, salad, fragrant couscous. "Delightful!" cried Julia, after tasting the dish. "Couscous is SO underrated!"

BEST DIRTY TRICK COMEUPPANCE

After a particularly good "Water Council" setup in the early years, Molly Saudek, Lilias Ide and Kate Podolec decided to get back at Rob. At midnight, they smeared ketchup all over Lilias's throat, to make it look like it had been cut, then snuck up to Rob's trailer door. As Lilias took in breath to let out a bloodcurdling scream, Rob's door popped open, he stuck his head out grinning—and doused the girls with two full buckets of water. The girls screamed for real, Rob calmly shut his door and just as calmly went back to sleep. "Around troupers," he explained later, "one must always be prepared."

ROMANCE IN THE RING

The most extended, loudest, most tumultuous roar ever heard in the Smirkus tent came from the audience in 1996. A brave young fellow approached Rob before one of the shows, wondering if he could propose to his girlfriend in the ring. Rob set it up: They chose the unsuspecting girlfriend as the volunteer in the "Park Bench" clown act and secretly whisked the man backstage into a clown nose. First Chris Grabher came out to woo her, then Richard Saudek. Then the actual boyfriend appeared, went down on one knee, took out the ring and she burst into tears as he popped the question. The music stopped and suddenly the audience realized this was for real. The cheering and roaring grew into a tent-shaking crescendo. It was mass confusion for 15 minutes as the audience wept and kissed one another and troupers threw confetti on everyone... Only after it calmed down did everyone realize the poor girl hadn't actually answered the proposal. Two days later, Rob ran into the man on the street and checked. The girl had had no choice, he replied: she'd said "Yes."

MOST CREATIVE USE OF MARSHMALLOWS

One day during the *Robin Hood* tour, bareback riding coach Tosca Zoppé and her husband, Jay Walther—who was that year's tent boss—spent lavishly on candy, makeup and other frou-frou goods for a party for the girls. This left Troy to entertain the boys in the church sanctuary where they were spending the night—with five dollars left in his pocket. So he used them to buy several bags of marshmallows, big and mini, and created the first "Marshmallow Olympics." The boys split into teams, and for two and a half hours, they competed. Who could stuff the most marshmallows in his mouth and still say "Chubby Bunny"? Who could make the highest marshmallow tower? Who could exhale a mini marshmallow farthest—from his nose? The competition was caught on film by the Disney crew that was following Smirkus that summer. But it never aired, out of concern that little kids might, in fact, try some of those stunts at home.

FUN CELEBRITY MOMENT II

In 1999, Hollywood producer Norman Lear brought comedian Dom DeLuise to the *Robin Hood* show. In the show, Rob, as Robin Hood, would pick an audience member to stand up and empty his pockets, to "give to the poor." That night, Rob chose Dom DeLuise, who stood up and declared that he had no money. Repartee between Robin and Dom revealed that for all his celebrity wealth, the actor carried no cash. Sheepishly, Dom offered Robin his credit card. "All I got is plastic—will that do in Sherwood?" he asked.

Clowns

Maybe it's a coincidence, but probably not: every Smirkus director—Rob Mermin, Jeff and Julie Jenkins, Troy Wunderle and Jesse Dryden—started out as a clown. Perhaps it's because clowns have to be able to do a little bit of everything, and are accustomed to thinking in terms of storyline and pacing.

So Smirkus takes clowning seriously—as an art form, not just a way to amuse the crowd between acts. "I firmly believed that the clowns needed to be the thread that bound the whole show together," says Jeff. "And the clowns could not simply be young kids with makeup and silly costumes. They had to be actors and communicators of the highest caliber. Great slapstick is like great ballet…It's wonderfully pleasing to the eye. The fact that it ends up with a belly laugh is icing on the cake."

Rob's contribution was to combine all these elements and to make sure there was a variety of clowning styles in the show: quick transition gags, longer classic European-style routines, partner gags, knockabout group slapstick, male and female clowns, and moments of gentle good humor.

"Over the years, Smirkus clown coaches have brought different slices of clowning's many traditions into the ring. Stewart Lippe introduced a brand of childlike simplicity and improvisation in the early years. Ted Lawrence and Jeff Jenkins brilliantly added the American element of classic Ringling-style slapstick. Jesse Dryden and Troy Wunderle bring a cartoonish humor and wacky theatricality to the clowning. It all requires teaching acrobatics to clowns, clowning to acrobats and adding mime, character and awareness of pacing and connecting directly to the audience." —Rob Mermin

SMIRKUS

SMIRKUS

"Wow, I can't believe we get away with this! If the world had only the smallest inkling of the unbelievable, unrivaled, unfathomable amount of fun we're having here at Smirkus, they'd just shut us down out of pure jealousy!"

—John Stork, former trouper, now circus performer

Laws of Smirkus Clown Society

—by Rob Mermin

A circus clown in the ring does not think he or she is funny. The clown doesn't find his situations humorous, though his very existence revolves around others laughing at how he handles his predicaments. He has a childlike curiosity about how the world works, together with a child's self-assured sense of how to do things—erroneously of course, but in absurdly creative ways. Inanimate objects have lives of their own: a stick is an umbrella, a sword, a toothbrush, a rocket.

The Smirkus clown doesn't make others look funny on purpose. He doesn't mock, but merely goes about business as he sees it, though he might parody other acts to lighten their heroics. He seems to be anarchic by nature, but really he just operates in a universe whose laws are different from ours. He functions unblinkingly, mischievous but not mean, without knowing any other way to behave except within the rules governing his own world.

The clown gets away with everything kids dream of: slapping, kicking in the butt, throwing water, poking authority in the nose, making a mess of things, falling down, being silly, acting smart-alecky. Yet it is imperative that the Smirkus clown behave without mockery, intentional malice, sarcasm or cynicism, but instead with fullness of heart.

"I've said for a long time that a good clown is the most talented person in the show. Because there are elements of clowning that just can't be taught, and because the only thing they're putting out in front of the audience is themselves. When an aerialist doesn't succeed, she gets to try it again and the audience will go wild when she does succeed. But a clown doesn't have that option. There's no second try. You can't redo a gag."

—Rachel Schiffer,
wire-walker and aerialist

CHAPTER SIX

LIFE AS A SMIRKO

Days and Nights
of High Adventure and
Low Comedy

I no longer perform, but the Smirkus experience shaped my life's work.
I credit Smirkus with teaching me to follow my dreams,
to value differences,
and to know that anything is possible.

—Sajana Blank, Smirko aerialist 1999-2004,
currently an administrator for AFS-USA International student exchanges

"What we're asking these kids to do is extraordinary. We're asking young people to move away from home, form a new family, work their bodies harder than most people in the world will ever know, put on an amazing show, travel all over and show it to everybody and still be happy and still be kids. It's pure passion for them."

—Willow Yonika, former trouper and head counselor in 2011 and 2012

"The year after I left Smirkus, I came back to visit. It was the last show, and they brought me into the ring to help do a chain, where four people would bend back and lay their heads on each other's knees. So there I am, with my head back, and all of a sudden, out of nowhere, I'm pied. They hadn't forgotten me! I felt loved!"

—Jade Kindar-Martin,
former trouper and coach,
now international sky-walker

One day, the troupers were practicing pyramids up in the loft. Casey Pickett was 13, and still small enough to be the kid at the top. The troupers were ready to have him climb up layers of legs, backs and shoulders to stand higher than he'd ever been—his head above the barn's rafters. He scrambled up and stood shakily on an equally shaky pair of shoulders. In the classic way that pyramids can, the whole thing began to buckle—someone gave way, which led someone else to crumple, which led the whole thing to collapse. Casey plummeted through the air. "I'm about to break something," he thought. "My summer's over." Suddenly, he stopped. Toby Ayer, the troupe's young giant of a juggler, had caught him. "It was like I was a damsel falling off a building and he was Batman," Casey says. "It was an amazing feat."

Smirkos hold each other up and they catch one another when they fall—sometimes literally, sometimes figuratively. Abby Suskin got word while on tour that her father had been in a bicycle accident; he died later as a result of his injuries. The summer of the accident, she spent her time traveling back and forth from the show to Montpelier, Vermont, to be with her family. "What's hard for people to understand is that there was no better place for me to be during that time than with Smirkus," she says. "I have this vivid memory, the first time I returned to the tour after having been gone for a few days, of these people who meant so much to me surrounding me with an overwhelming feeling of love."

Patrick Mannion's life turned around when the family of another trouper, Alex Friedlander-Moore, took him in. Pat grew up in a blue-collar Massachusetts town with a single mom, and though he was a Smirkus mainstay during the summer, he struggled at home—kicked off the school bus for misbehaving, brought home by the police for fighting. "I'd go to Smirkus and feel like I'd gained all this confidence," he says, "and then go home and just count down until the next summer when I could live again. I was floundering." That was when the Friedlander-Moores offered him a place to stay and to send

him to a nearby school to learn culinary arts. "They ate dinner together as a family every night, which I'd never experienced, and they made it clear that your responsibilities were important, whether it was school or practicing for soccer," says Pat, who is now a chef as well as a circus performer in Chicago. "It just completely changed my life."

Of course, it is also true that Smirko guys like to sneak out of their trailers in the dead of night and scratch eerily on the side of the girls' trailer with a fork, or come up with ever more ingenious ways to pie someone on his or her birthday, or even, as happened once

"For a while, when I was getting into my teens, Smirkus was the strongest support I had. I remember saying at a closing meeting, 'My life right now is so rocky, but I know that I'll always have Smirkus and this community and this family.' To this day, I consider it one of the most solid things in my life."

—Tristan Cunningham,
former trouper,
now professional actor/clown

"At my audition, they put people through the acrobatic stuff, like forward rolls and cartwheels. I'd never done any gymnastics, other than starting at the top of a hill and doing somersaults down it. So they started out with forward rolls, and it wasn't pretty but I did it. Then we moved on to cartwheels, and I at least knew the basic idea. Then they asked those who could do a back handspring to step forward. Before anyone could stop me, I flung myself in the air and landed flat on my face. Rob blanched. I stood up and did my style and walked off, humiliated. That was apparently enough to land me a spot in the troupe!"

—Porter Lontz-Underhill,
former trouper, now film
& tv production professional

in the early years, suspend a duct-taped fellow-trouper upside down from the rigging in the tent. One year, after the clowns created their own separate Clown Alley in imitation of Ringling, another group took over a rented Ryder truck and created Punk Alley, to which a group of girls responded by creating Diva Alley—which led to the clowns rigging the punks' costumes at the top of the tent, the divas running a spider web of string around the punks' Ryder, and finally, the clowns capturing one of the punks, taping him to a chair in the truck and then lying in wait with buckets of water for when the rest of the punks came upon him.

Yet what many Smirkus troupers remember most clearly is the rooted sense of togetherness and acceptance they found with one another. "The hardest thing I ever had to do at Smirkus," says Dan Brown, "was leave Smirkus."

So years after they move on, Smirkos still lean on one another for support. They cluster in the same few cities or travel long distances to see each other perform, they show up at auditions, they check in on the tour, they phone and write and spend hours on social networks and seize every chance they can to visit. Even troupers who never overlapped in their careers at Smirkus bond over their common spark, especially if they find themselves performing together later in life. "There's this mentality about other Smirkos," says Tristan Cunningham. "You know they're reliable. You know they're experienced. And you know they can work with anybody."

Since the day Smirkus set up Old Blue, the troupers chosen for the tour have made for an intriguing mix of characters. They have been prima donnas and hooligans, bookworms and punks, misfits, cheerleaders, hard workers and pranksters. Some come from calm families, others from turbulent homes they're desperate to escape. There are kids who get the best training money can buy, and others who scrape together a jerry-built practice apparatus. What unites them all is having fallen in love with the circus.

It takes a lot to get into Smirkus these days. Hundreds of kids send in audition videos, which are pared down by Troy and Jesse to just a handful; returning troupers get a pass on that part. But they, along with the newcomers, have to go through two grueling days of live auditions, which include a three-minute act, strength and acrobatic assessments, improvisations and an interview. The routines are generally of such high quality that old-time Smirkos—even the ones who've grown into sought-after circus performers—are convinced that they would never get in if their 14-year-old self had to audition now.

Which could be true. Though the bar got higher throughout the '90s as Smirkos' abilities grew, until about 2001 you could still show up unannounced. There was a tumbling assessment, and showing skill didn't hurt—acrobatics, a magic trick, walking on your hands—but especially in the earlier years Rob, Stewart and Alla were after more than technical ability.

"I was looking for the impressively skilled, the oddball talent, the rebel with spirit, the misfit with secret dreams."

I was looking for the impressively skilled, the oddball talent, the rebel with spirit, the misfit with secret dreams. Sometimes you could see it in their eyes, or a hint in something they said, or maybe a certain body language that communicated a private yearning. Often the quietest kid, the one observing the more outgoing ones in action, was the one I took a chance on. In them I recognized myself as a kid. And the ones who didn't quite fit in were a good balance to the well-adjusted, well-off, extra-trained kids who already excelled.

In the early years I found talent wherever I could. I drove down to Connecticut to audition Nolan Haims in a parking lot after he had read about the program in the papers and written to me. He could ride a unicycle, juggle and do magic tricks. Good enough! I interviewed Leo Sblendorio in his home in Great Barrington, Massachusetts, where he rode his unicycle around the kitchen while playing a fiddle, accompanied by his dad on accordion, while I sipped tea. Sign him up!

Whenever I did school residencies during the year I would keep an eye out for talented kids, especially those with gymnastic and athletic abilities. I also liked the kids who seemed to be out of place, the classroom trouble-makers: they had good clown potential. Clowning would give these kids permission to make fun of authority and buck conformity, as well as to find their own responsible role in the unconventional environment of circus.

Kids come to auditions carrying two metaphorical suitcases, one in each hand. One suitcase contains learned skills, the other suitcase contains natural talents. Kids walk in "unbalanced," since one suitcase is usually filled with more than the other. The fulcrum is the kid: he or she is filled with a personality that, when added to either suitcase, provides the necessary balance. Personality and character were more important to me than specific skills: skills can always be learned, but character is natural.

In the early years, Smirkus couldn't be choosy about technical ability, because there weren't that many kids with circus skills. They did gymnastics or dance or taught themselves to juggle, but as longtime trouper Rachel Schiffer says, "There was nowhere to do circus during the year; no one even knew it was something you could do after school." That changed as circus-training facilities sprang up around the country—and as Smirkus troupers themselves, beginning in the 1990s, began training year-round wherever they lived and could find or make improvised rigging. Coaches like Alla, Zina and Volodya Avgustov routinely made themselves available in Vermont during the winter for troupers to visit and brush up, a tradition carried on over the years by former and current coaches like Bill Forchion, Elsie Smith and Serenity Smith Forchion, and Sellam Ouahabi.

In a sense, Smirkus has developed two approaches to meeting its needs in the ring. It grows its own talent—it has now produced several generations of troupers who came in with rudimentary skills and left as qualified professionals—and it goes out and finds it.

By 1999, its second generation of homegrown talent—crowd-pleasing performers like Sam Johnson, Richard Saudek, Doug Bair, Chris Grabher, Andrew Adams, Lisa Taylor-Parisi and Vanessa Lind—had moved on, leaving a huge void at the same time that the circus's artistic ambitions were growing. Smirkus was lucky, though. Ozzie had encountered a knot of talented kids who went to a Waldorf school in New Hampshire and he convinced their parents to let them audition for the 1999 tour. They were part of a school-based troupe run by an accomplished circus coach in central New Hampshire, Jackie Davis, and they trained and performed year-round. The McKeeman twins, Kerren and Kaleen; siblings David and Thora Graham; Tobin Renwick, Jacob Skeffington and Willow Yonika arrived at Smirkus as strong jugglers, competent acrobats and promising aerialists, and—together with veteran returning troupers like Rachel Schiffer and Francey Grund—quickly helped form the core of the next few years' troupes. "They were so motivated, and

"The love of your circus became a part of me—every day there is always something that reminds me of the spirit and love which your circus provided. May the Spirit fly and the Dream soar forever."

—Sam Pashe,
Sioux Nation trouper,
from a letter to Rob

they were constantly working and improving," remembers Francey. "That community really helped move everyone's skills forward."

These days growing interest in circus is providing Smirkus with an ever increasing pool of talent from all over America. But from the beginning, Rob searched restlessly for troupers from outside New England. The first imports were a group from The Great American Circus, a YMCA-run after-school circus program in California. Then came the Russians and Latvians, the Mongolian contortionists, the Chinese equilibrists and, thanks to a connection Jeff and Julie had made, the Chicago Boyz acrobats.

Sometimes, Rob's search for interesting troupers would take him far afield. He spent a year negotiating with Ringling Bros. and Barnum & Bailey executives to bring teens from 10 Native American nations to Smirkus. This sprang from a contract Alla had with Ringling, to create an act with Indians for their show—she and Rob figured the performers could get their show legs by touring with Smirkus, and then move on to Ringling.

It was amusing to negotiate over the winter in the Greensboro farmhouse with Indian chiefs, Ringling vice-presidents and Russian circus directors sitting around sipping tea with maple syrup. Everyone had an agenda. There were 20 pages of fine-print contract from Ringling, which were indecipherable and unacceptable to me. Creative control by the Indians was unacceptable to Ringling. Boye Ladd, a member of the Ho Chunk and Zuni Indian nations, was a mediator for the Indian chiefs. By summer, revisions had gone back and forth between Ringling and the Indians with no truce. So I kept the Indian group training and performing with us all summer, and soon the Smirkus season was over...while Ringling and the Indians haggled for the next year.

TRAINING

What most spectators don't fully appreciate about circus training is that it hurts—the tightwire is coiled steel and you can't wear thick soles to protect your feet; the pole digs deep into muscles and tendons; the trapeze, lyra and cradle gouge knees, arms, shoulders and backs, and the ropes that hold them can burn a livid welt with a second's inattention. Kids with gymnastics training can move loosely and fluidly down a training mat, but others get stuck in awkward poses in the middle of a basic forward roll and need help finishing it. As Troy Wunderle says, "That's the thing about circus—if you're the best juggler, you're probably not the best tumbler. It keeps you humble."

Yet in spite of this, troupers cheerfully learn not only the technical skills they'll need to perfect an act, but also to choreograph it, work in frictionless tandem with their partners and make it all look as easy as an afterthought. And here's the interesting thing: this is what makes them happy. "The thread that unites us all is that we revel in doing

Sacred Ground

"My mother was at the wheel when we came out of the woods and into the hayfields. Something there caught my eye: two shirtless Native American boys with long hair walking through the golden, waist-deep hay. They were deep in conversation but looked peaceful. But Native American reservations are amongst the poorest communities in the Americas, and to call these guys tough is an understatement. Their attitude was a way of survival back home. Their hard looks seemed to convey the message, "What do you want from me?" It took all of training and into the tour before they realized what we wanted from them: fun. On stage, though, what they brought to Smirkus was arguably the most powerful and spiritual performances to grace the ring. Old Blue became sacred ground. By the end of the summer we had created lasting bonds. The two boys I'd seen walking in the field, brothers Sam and John Pashe, became Smirkus staples as they returned for many summers."

—Sam Johnson

Boss Clown Olympics

Sunbathers on the Lake Champlain beach in Plattsburgh, NY were dumbfounded one July day in 2010 to see a strapping, redheaded young woman and a young man with a rubbery face and uncannily expressive eyebrows trying to outdo each other prat-falling into the water. What followed was even more bewildering: the two got thoroughly covered in sand as they did a forward-roll race across the beach, then pied themselves in the face, then stood there, wet and sandy, as they got quizzed on the names of professional clowns, the names of Circus Smirkus clowns and the correct ordering numbers for clown noses. This was the first annual **Boss Clown Olympics** to choose the new lead member of Smirkus's Clown Alley. In one corner: Frances Tiffin. In the other: Jared Mongeau. They went toe-to-toe on the quizzes, made pies and put on clown makeup without a mirror. The winner was chosen by who got the loudest cheers—and it was a dead tie. They shared the Boss Clown title for the rest of the tour. These days they can still be found together, entertaining audiences as clowns for Ringling.

things that people tell us are not possible or you can't do—and doing them in a way that looks effortless and graceful," says Francey Grund. At Smirkus, drive and intensity and a deep pleasure in mastering the mechanics of art are the common coin, the force that drives adults and kids alike and binds them together.

HOMESTAYS

Keeping a circus on the road is hard work, not least because you have to figure out where people are going to sleep. Early on, Smirkus relied heavily on church basements and school gymnasiums, but it quickly developed the system of "homestays" that now marks its travels. In every town where it sets up, local residents kindly open their homes to troupers. For many of the troupers, homestays are a defining experience. "Don't just write a note saying 'Thank you for having me,'" Rob would say. "Do something creative. Leave a note inside the fridge saying, 'Thanks, I loved your food.' Leave a note on the pillows, 'Thanks for the bed.' Leave notes hidden around the house so they'll be finding them for days—they'll remember you forever!"

But homestays are also, for many troupers, their first lesson in being social out in the world at large. "They are a huge part of what sculpted me," says Dan Brown. "You're forced to go into this random family's home and experience their way of life for a few days. Sometimes it's great, and sometimes it's not, but you're forced to interact with so many different people—you're just a teenager, and here you are with grownups just carrying on full conversations. I got people skills that I'll carry with me the rest of my life." Some troupers stay with the same family year after year—they watch their hosts' children grow up, teach them juggling and acrobatics, and stay in touch for years afterward.

The result is that the communities Smirkus visits come to feel a part of it. "Even though you're just an outsider, you get connected to those kids," says Betsy Van Gemeren, who opened her home in Simsbury, Connecticut, to Smirkus troupers when the tour passed through. "You get to be part of the Smirkus family—they hug you with their homestays, and then you never let go."

As Elsie Smith puts it, "It's a huge community bonding experience. Not only is the circus coming to town, but *your* circus is coming to town!"

RESPONSIBILITY AND DISCIPLINE

On opening night of the *Robin Hood* show in 1999, just a few minutes after the opening *charivari*, a transformer blew and the show lost power. It was getting dark. With almost no direction from the coaches, troupers who weren't in the ring busied themselves rolling up tent sides to allow in more light; jugglers snatched up their fire torches, lit them and handed them out to fellow troupers, who took turns standing at the edge of the ring to keep the show lit; their parents ran up into the field where cars were parked, drove down and ringed the tent with their headlights.

There is a long tradition in circus, especially with small mud shows, of everyone pitching in. Performers tote tent stakes and help stitch costumes. Souvenir sellers help unload trucks. Administrators hawk water and cotton candy in the tent. "In the same show early on I went from being the first Smirko with a solo act to being the head of the zebra in the next act," remembers Jade Kindar-Martin. "That's what Smirkus was: being the star in one act, having a supporting part in the next, and then scrubbing pots and pans after the show."

Keeping troupers focused on this all-for-one-and-one-for-all spirit isn't always easy, and it is a particularly tough balancing act to make sure they have the room to be teenagers while not violating the communal discipline needed to keep a show on the road and six or seven dozen people living in harmony cheek-by-jowl. It begins with the Trouper Contract, which everyone who joins the troupe must sign, but it also takes some creative parenting. The approach Smirkus has developed over time, as Josh Shack sums it up, is "You plant seeds instead of pointing fingers."

The best individual discipline is not extra chores, but to be temporarily taken out of an act or, in extreme circumstances, out of the show. Just the threat of this last punishment has been enough over the years to straighten wayward minds.

Once, the troupers decided to accept discipline as a group for the disruptive, erratic behavior of a few. I appreciated the solidarity of the idea, but I didn't know how to discipline the whole company. I said they should discuss it themselves, find suitable measures, and I'd be back in 10 minutes to hear it.

Their solution, announced by spokesman Cris Clark, was perfect. Rather than taking away something limited like mere personal privileges, they thought it would be best to add something positive and of lasting benefit to the circus. So they made a list and spent a happy, productive afternoon washing the trucks, weeding the flower garden, scrubbing dirty tent walls and painting props. We have learned to respect the troupers' right to make mistakes, their acceptance of consequences and their creative notions of self-discipline and fair play.

For many years, Ozzie Henchel joined Rob in keeping troupers pointed in the right direction. "Ozzie didn't say, 'You did this wrong!'" says Pat Mannion. "It was the way he lived and the stories he told and the positive things he pointed out. He respected us and treated us like real people, not like kids. Most of the adults at Smirkus did that: just because you were small and a kid didn't mean they treated you like a child."

As for Rob, probably the classic illustration of his approach came one year when the troupers were staying in dorms at Concord Academy. Several of the girls stayed up late sharing a cigarette—an offense that might get them kicked out of Smirkus. Two of them

"Very talented young people don't always translate into people who have the guts and desire to become performers. What it takes to be a performer is someone who can work through when it's not fun anymore: when a trick scares you, or your body hurts and you're sore and tired and don't want to get out of bed. The ones who can get past that are the ones who will succeed."

—Serenity Smith Forchion, aerial coach

"I learned a coach trick from Bat: 'One more time!' never means one more time. It's more like 20 more times. But you'd say, 'Well, I can push myself one more time,' and then inevitably it would be an hour later and you'd still be doing it."

—Francey Grund, former trouper

were clearly visible in the upstairs window when a male head emerged from the window right below and said, calmly, "Ladies! Put the cigarette out and go to bed."

"All the girls lost it," recalls Francey Grund, "but Lisa and I said, 'OK, he saw us. We'll take the fall for everyone.' We didn't sleep a wink that night—we were bawling our eyes out, thinking, 'OK, it's over, we're going home... How could we threaten the best thing we ever had for a cigarette?'"

The next morning, a counselor told them that Rob wanted to see them. Francey and Lisa got to the tent site and busied themselves doing other things to put off the inevitable, but eventually, they walked over to Rob. "We were both wrecks," says Francey, "and as we got closer and closer, Rob played along with us for a minute, giving us this face and shaking his head. And we come up with this elaborate story..." Rob listened patiently, waiting to see how fanciful their story would get. Finally, he looked down at the ground, impassively, then looked at them and asked, "So, did you like it? What brand was it?" The girls were flabbergasted. Then he told them about being 12 years old, caught smoking with his older brother

Teen Romance

A conversation with Alumni Smirkos:

Rob: I get asked all the time by adults, "How do you deal with sexuality? These kids are beautiful! They're touching each other and holding each other and lifting each other. And they're healthy and young and teens!" Now, you guys have always told me, "What? We're too tired! Besides, we think of ourselves as brothers and sisters." Really, how true is that?

Chris Grabher: First of all, look, we're all teenagers, right? So we're going to go through what teenagers go through. But all that stuff—being in good shape, touching each other—all of that was purely related to the show, it was work. And I'll be honest with you, whether we were doing gymnastics or pyramids or lifting, it was all business. Teenage romance didn't happen when we were working.

Francey Grund: What made adults uncomfortable was that working that closely together led to an easy physical closeness backstage. It wasn't sexual...There aren't normal boundaries at Smirkus. Once you've crossed over that [touching] boundary in the ring, then why would you all of a sudden stay three feet away from each other outside the ring?

by their father, who then bought a pack of every brand available and made his sons smoke them all nonstop. They never touched a cigarette again.

With that, he let them go. Their punishment, he told them later, was that they'd spent the entire night crying, in fear of what they were in danger of losing. "That," he said, "was plenty."

Teen romance will appear, and it can be a chance for staff to discuss sensitive issues with the troupers. Not just the confusion of sexuality, but about attraction; about caring for another person; about deep friendships, kindness, sensitivity—and being aware of the effect of your behavior on others. To ignore teen romance, or suppress it outright, is to encourage the secretive side of it. The spirit of being able to confide in another, and to be of help figuring out life issues, is part of the program here.

Traditions

PANIC

On a mid-June evening, once the troupers have gotten into the rhythm of training, Trailerville—the outdoor trouper courtyard at headquarters—becomes center ring. The staff and crew drag over whatever chairs they can find, line them up in the field and form the audience for a spirited game of Panic.

Panic is a bigger, bolder scavenger hunt. Each trailer-full of troupers forms a team. Their job is to find whatever item the game's "caller" tells them to search for and be the first back to the trailer with it. The sillier the item, the better. The game requires:

• in-depth knowledge—about, say, which staffer likes a particular kind of jelly bean and where she keeps her stash, or where a costume from 20 years ago can be found;
• quick reactions and a fast pair of legs—if the "item" is a freshly showered Smirko, you want to be the first Smirko to the showers;
• and a conniving, ruthless mind, the kind that would think to lock the trouper who beat you to that jelly bean in the office where he found it, for instance, or would stoop to bribing the judges with their favorite kinds of chocolate.

A lot of Smirkos got interested in circus because they wanted to be athletic without being competitive. Panic brings out their inner dog-eat-dog.

THE BANQUET

In the blue-and-yellow-striped Academy tent, where troupers just spent the day sweating through acrobatics and Chinese-pole training, the white tablecloths are spread and the tables laid end-to-end, topped with candelabra and good silverware. For a genteel few hours during the second week of training, just as exhausted muscles are setting in, the rough-and-tumble daily life of the circus is forgotten.

Everyone chips in to help. Staff and troupers collect wildflowers, decorate the tent and set up the candles and place settings. Troupers help the chefs chop vegetables or get ready to serve as tuxedo-clad waiters. The chefs spend all day in the pie car, pulling out every culinary stop they can dream up: Asian dumplings, spring rolls, cantaloupe *granita*, dates stuffed with goat cheese, prosciutto-wrapped melon, baked apple puff pastries, baked Alaska—and that's just one year's menu! Eventually, staff and troupers alike repair to their bunks to get dressed, the women and girls in flowing dresses (except for the occasional year when it's the boys who don dresses and makeup), the men and boys in their natty best. Everyone sits down to an evening of memorable food, fine speeches of appreciation and a last, fleeting taste of elegance before the grueling final push to Opening Day begins.

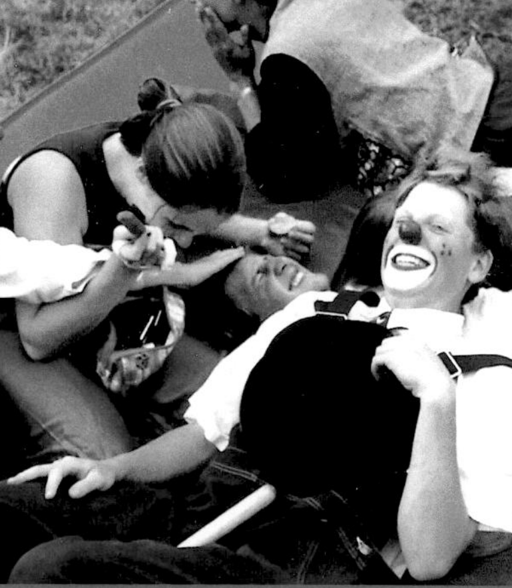

COUNCIL MEETING

Each night during training, not long after dinner, someone rings the bell on the porch of the old farmhouse and the call goes out over Smirkus-land: "Council! Council!" Troupers and adults alike make their way to the barn loft, where whoever's running the meeting will bang the council stick—an old circus prop—for attention, light a candle, and for the next hour or so they'll talk over everything that needs a group conversation.

Council began as a time to gather the company, sit in the barn and just talk at the end of the day. I wanted to create a place to discuss not only rehearsal and show issues, but to take a break from training and learn new things about each other. I often began council with a favorite piece of classical music, or a poem, introducing some bit of culture other than circus. I encouraged the troupe to share something of their personal interests each night. Practical daily issues that needed addressing were gotten out of the way early and became known as Pots & Pans, since they usually involved chores. Then we could move on to larger life issues. There were discussions about romance, home life, a parent who was seriously ill. It was always gratifying to witness the large age range of youth speaking to each other and to the adults as real friends and partners, with the mutual respect garnered by shared emotional experience. The company still hashes out issues at council meetings today, but the most emotional conversations now come at the end of the tour, as troupers mull over the summer's experiences at the "Final Council" before everyone heads home.

Joke Show!

All through the *Frontpage Follies* tour, clowns Colin Miclon and Chase Culp performed a popular act with dueling typewriters—which required carefully timed *clacks* and *dings* from the sound-effects booth. During one show at the end of tour, Colin raised his hand dramatically to hit his typewriter key, lowered it... and out came a *Mooooo*. He looked down at his typewriter, confused, and tried again. This time it was an antique car's *Beep Beep*. It was the Joke Show!

Anything can happen during Joke Show. Native American dancers in full regalia wear Groucho Marx glasses. Costumes from previous years' shows make an unexpected reappearance. The smallest troupers do yeoman's work—little Sian Flatt taking 6'5" Toby Ayer's place as Little John in his quarterstaff battle with Robin Hood; the entire troupe prances through the ring, wearing animal heads, toting old props, walking their dogs.

Rob: In my years in Copenhagen there was a tradition of the annual joke show in the middle of the season. I continued this tradition religiously at Smirkus, scheduling it for the end of the tour. The hometown audience came to relish the antics with anticipation. Anyone—performer or crew—was allowed to pull out the practical jokes with the stipulation that the prank would not disrupt the show itself or the audience's enjoyment of it.

One year, I told the troupers a minute before showtime that they should be ready with their props because I was going to change the order of the show without warning—the only way they would know if their act was on next would be to listen to the music. I had no intention of actually doing it until I saw their alarmed faces and I just KNEW it must be done! Two minutes into the trapeze act I changed to the jugglers' music. Suddenly the curtain opened and out ran six frantic jugglers under the confused trapeze girls. As the jugglers began throwing clubs in the air, I switched to the clown music and the jugglers froze, looked around in panic and ran out, bumping into the clowns. After a couple minutes of this hilarious chaos I stopped the show and we started again from the top, correctly. Yes, I broke my own rules. It was a riotous prank that only the director was allowed to pull off.

Above:
Jade Kindar-Martin, skywalker

Never Look Down

In 1999, the Robin Hood year, Rob Gurwitt spent the summer following Smirkus for a story that ran the next year in DoubleTake *magazine. He caught not just the hard work that goes into training, but a Smirkus passing-of-the-torch: Jade Kindar-Martin's return as a coach to teach highwire-walking skills to a new generation. From the* DoubleTake *article:*

Across the center of the *Chapiteau*, 15 feet overhead, a tightwire runs from stanchion to stanchion and then out between flaps to where it is anchored by four-foot iron stakes driven into the soaking ground. The wire was put up yesterday, and now Rachel Schiffer and Willow Yonika are trying their first full practice session on it. The opening show is just a week from tomorrow.

Willow goes up first. She is dressed in a thin gray leotard; her body, slender and supple, suits her name. The wire coach, Jade Kindar-Martin, helps her into a climber's harness and tightens it so firmly she winces. He watches as she climbs one of the masts supporting the tent, reaches the wire and clips a safety cable onto the harness. Tentatively, she slides one foot out onto the wire. "Don't look at your feet!" Jade calls. For the last week and a half, Willow and Rachel have been practicing on wires a foot or two from the ground. They've learned to jump, run, kneel, turn and do a split. They've learned to grip the wire with their feet, to fight for their balance and to understand what it means to be vertical in a way that nothing else could possibly teach them. They've learned never to look down: to fix their eyes at the far end of the wire and feel their next step by sliding their foot.

Up this high, it all has to be relearned. Willow, who on the low wire was a prodigy of balance, steps and slides across the much longer high wire and then falters. She gingerly makes her way back to the mast. "I don't feel like I can do tricks up there," she announces.

Rachel falls on her first step. It is a hard shift to make, that small step from the generous security of the mast to the unforgiving emptiness along the wire. She swings out across the ring, held by the "lunge"—the safety cable—then swings back to the mast.

"I don't ever want to see you just give up like that," Jade tells her.
"That first step's *hard*!" she protests.
Jade softens. "Take a couple of minutes to find your balance. And breathe," he says, drawing the word out.

She tries, squaring herself, loosening her stance, but she falls again. This time, she grabs the wire

Rachel Schiffer, **left;** Willow Yonika, **right. Below:** Rachel, Willow and Jade in *Robin Hood*

and hoists herself back on. She stands, does a half turn and slips off. Jade, who is holding the other end of the lunge, lowers her to the wire, where she sits and catches her breath. "Did you guys think a week ago when you first got on the wire that you could walk this high?" Jade asks. "No," Rachel admits.

"Right," he says. "Whatever you think is impossible is not impossible. It's *completely* possible."

But at this moment, for Rachel, it's not. Four more times she tries standing up, but each time some subtle force pulls her away and she sprawls out into the air. Finally, she manages to get up, walk back to the mast, and climb down. She sits on the ring curb, alone and mute, huddled against the cold, her eyes lacking their customary flash. For the first time in two weeks, Rachel looks like just what she is: a 15-year-old girl who is discovering the limits of her will.

The practice wears on. Willow grows more confident, her walk looser, her turns steadier. She's getting her bearings at the new height. Rachel, too, seems surer the second time up, more in command. "That's the Rachel I know!" Jade calls. She nails her turns, fights for her balance and wins, even runs once when Jade urges her to try. But then comes her third try. She starts out confidently, then feels the lunge tugging at her back and loses her concentration. She grips the wire, tries to stand, and falls. She tries rising from her knees and falls. Nothing works, so she falls. The lunge holds her each time, but it's exhausting and the wire is merciless, a bruising steel-hard line with nothing to grab onto above, nothing below it to push off from, nothing to its side to lean on so that her muscles can find a moment's rest. Finally, Jade says softly, "Come on down, Rachel."

This would be the moment for her to give in, to allow herself to be lowered by the lunge. But with a tight voice, Rachel asks if she can try walking to the mast. Shakily, she steps and slides until, three feet from the end, she tilts to the side, trying desperately to shift her upper body back over the wire.

"Keep moving!" Jade yells. "Keep moving! Keep moving!"

She can't. She slips off, swings out and back across the ring, and gets lowered to the ground. As her feet touch, a deep sob comes bursting out and she makes her way to the ring curb, dropping next to Willow, weeping. A couple of Smirkus troupers who'd wandered into the tent look panicked, turn, and leave. Jade lets Rachel cry for a few moments, then walks over, kneels at her feet, and starts talking to her quietly.

Both Willow and Rachel overcame these early struggles and their act became one of the highlights of the show—and the only time in its history Smirkus has used a high wire. After Smirkus, Rachel went on to become a star wire-walker herself; Willow trained as a nurse and, in 2011 and 2012, returned as Smirkus's head counselor.

Lifting the Curtain

Just trying to list the unique acts that have appeared in the Smirkus ring over the years would take half this book. Your tastes run to the lyrical? There was the juggling adagio featuring Toby Ayer and Russian Anastassia Tarassova in 1994's *Houdini Lives!*—based on Picasso's "Girl on a Ball," with classical music by Gabriel Fauré. Or the moment in 1998's Rock 'n' Roll Tour when circus legend Alberto Zoppé sat on the ring curb with Rob reminiscing about his first act as a boy for his family's circus in Italy, while behind him Sam Johnson was revealed on a slackwire, reproducing Alberto's memories.

For gasp-inducing wonder, you could take any of Rachel Schiffer's back handsprings off the cradle, in which she arched out over empty space before plunging head down to where her "catcher" had risen to grasp her wrists; or the sweet, muscular straps *pas de deux* in 2002's *Legends of the Wild West*, which showcased the strength and grace of Dan Brown and Kaleen McKeeman as they reached the verge of their careers as performers; or Mason Ames and Alex Friedlander-Moore's euphoric and poignant duo acrobatic act in 2005's *Pinocchio*.

And then, of course, there are the clown acts: Zelda the Zebra, a classic comedy two-person animal costume remembered for finishing the act by dropping large striped foam poops as it exited; or "The Boxing Match" between Toby The Terrible (6'5") and little Chris The Crusher (not much over 4' at the time) in a slapstick act that got all little kids cheering over bigger bullies; or the cartoonish play among Jacob Tischler's wolf, Anna Conway's hare and Shea Vaccaro's tortoise in 2009's *Smirkus Ever After*—memorable especially for the tortoise's slow-motion pantsing of the wolf; or Troy Wunderle's 2011 battle over a newspaper and a chair with his daughter Arianna, with tiny Arianna, of course, winning to hoots of delight from the littlest kids crowded around the ring curb.

Acts come together in any number of ways, some of which might surprise you...

THE GREAT VANESSA

Struggling to regain his balance as he recovers from his broken neck, Rob decides to learn to stand on five rola bolas—the rolling cylinders that no one in his right mind would try to climb atop. "This was the wonderful paradox of it: to find the center of balance, you had constantly to go off it," Rob remembers. He masters his newfound skill, then weaves it into an act. In the ring, Vanessa Lind balances on three stacked rola bolas, finishes to thunderous applause and shakes hands around the audience. In the background, assistant Robbo's hat gets caught in the safety wire high in the air. The only way to get it is to stack *five* rola bolas on milk crates and climb up. He snags his hat just as the ringmaster spies him and orders him out for disrupting the show. "It reminds us that sometimes, in life as on the stage, the most remarkable and subtle person is not the one in the limelight," enthuses Rob's high school English teacher.

JAILHOUSE ROCK

For 1998's *Rock 'n' Roll* Tour, Alla wants a huge ensemble "Spanish Web" act, on eight ropes slung from an extended cradle. The troupe trains on it for a couple of weeks, but Alla can't quite figure out where they're headed. Until Rob hands her a copy of Elvis Presley's "Jailhouse Rock." Suddenly she sees the ropes as the bars of a jail, with the performers unexpectedly "freed" by the music. The result is a kinetic blend of Old World circus technique and boisterous American spirit as the webs fill with a rollicking mass of troupers climbing, swinging, hanging upside-down and right-side-up in a buoyant scene where Elvis himself appears.

BUCKET-SLINGERS

The day before the opening of 2002's *Legends of the Wild West,* Ryan Combs and Sam Brown are still looking for one more clown act. They notice each other outside the house after lunch. Each is eating a cookie. They square off and finish them, trading contemptuous bites as if in a duel. By the time they get to the tent, they've decided to put the faceoff in the show—only using water. The result is an inspired variety of sprays, streams, spurts and sprinklers, mixed with such underhanded playfulness and perfect timing that audiences are helpless with laughter. "The hardest thing was that Ryan would be making these hysterical faces," says Sam, "and I'd have a bunch of water in my mouth and be trying not to laugh."

EMILY

It's opening night for *Legends of the Wild West.* Troy Wunderle is playing the sheriff of Greensboro Gulch. To create a "quiet moment," he'll pull a child from the audience and teach her to spin a trick rope. Only tonight, the first two girls he approaches shake their heads "no." Seeing this, Troy's daughter Emily, not even two years old, slides off her mom's lap in the bleachers, hoists herself over the ring curb and waddles up to Troy in the ring. Taken aback, he places a bandanna over her neck. It slides down to her waist. Together, they stand in the ring spinning the lasso while the audience cheers and Troy tears up. Smirkus will continue the long circus tradition of children working with their parents in the ring.

THE SWING

The act itself is pretty simple—Kia Eastman as Alice and Isabel Patrowicz as the rabbit in a duo trapeze act for 2004's *Smirkus Through the Looking Glass.* But there's a vulnerable innocence that reminds adults in the audience of their own passage out of childhood. It emerges as Julie Jenkins notices that Isabel and Kia are coming into their own as adolescents and performers, but don't yet have the polish or strength they'll develop in later years. "We got them at this very sweet moment, when they didn't fit as little girls anymore, but they weren't young women yet," Julie says. "They were just on the verge, and that's what showed up in the ring."

THE PASS

Coaching the wire act for 2005's *Pinocchio,* Molly Saudek remembers how Stewart built *esprit de corps* among the jugglers when she was a trouper. So she does the same thing, encouraging her four wire-walkers to work together outside regular practice times, placing little bets on tricks, taking them out to brunch if they nail a hard trick three times in a row. The result is a signature wire act, constantly in motion, including a breathtakingly difficult "pass," in which Jacob Sherry and Patrick Tobin approach each other along the wire and, in a flash, trade places. The foursome—it also includes Jacob Bloom and Abby Suskin—become a memorably tight-knit team. Says Molly, "They really loved each other by the end of the tour."

HOW DO YOU GET TO THE FESTIVAL MONDIAL...?

Practice. Hours and hours of practice. Brothers Nate and Jacob Stein-Sharpe put together a jaw-dropping display of diabolo artistry for *Tropical Vacation.* They start with a single diabolo, showcasing steals, intricate stickwork, lightning-quick passes and an endearing showmanship that is by turns balletic and clownlike. In their hands, the diabolo takes on a life of its own. They build to two diabolos, then three, and finally wind up pass-juggling five diabolos between them—a feat that puts them in world-class company. That year, they're the only Americans invited to the Festival Mondial du Cirque de Demain in Paris.

Ozzie!

The first time Smirkus traveled to Nantucket, Ozzie Henchel stayed up all night. The ferry couldn't handle the circus's dozen vehicles all at once, so they had to be sent out at different intervals. And Ozzie, in charge of driving the troupers there, had to hope that no mishaps or breakdowns threw a wrench into his finely wrought schedule.

"The troupers and I were on our way to Nantucket," he remembers, "and when I got the message, 'The tent crew is on the ferry,' as much as I'm not a tech guy I pulled that pager thing off my belt and kissed it!"

The return trip was less congenial. If you've ever ridden the Nantucket ferry, you know it doesn't wait for stragglers. But while Ozzie and the troupers made it on board for their scheduled departure, the cook bus—which was supposed to be on the same ferry—did not. The ferry captain was ready to go. He and Ozzie squared off, browbeating each other as the troupers looked on, wide-eyed. Twenty minutes went by. Furious, the captain began untying the ferry. Suddenly, the cook bus hove into sight... on the back of a tow truck. Now the captain was livid, because to get the cook bus on, the tow truck would have to back it into place, causing yet more delay. But then he looked at Ozzie. With an unprintable exclamation, he got the bus settled and the ferry moving.

For 13 seasons, this was what Ozzie did. "He could fix anything, he could make anything, he could withstand anything, he could solve any problem," says Barb Baird, an early head counselor. "And he always did it with aplomb." Or as Chris Grabher puts it, "He would plug the generator's power cables into his ears if he had to, to make the show go."

Rob and Ozzie hit it off from the beginning. Rob needed a right-hand guy, someone he trusted who bought his vision for what Smirkus could be and would help get it there. So Ozzie became its guardian spirit along with Rob—tough, caring, fiercely protective of Smirkus, Rob and the troupers. It was not an easy life during the summer. Smirkus had bought an old bus for Ozzie to drive the troupers in—the first in a series of what became known as "the Oz bus"—and it was hot and noisy...and also Ozzie's home; he slept on the floor. The crew got to sleep on top of the rented Ryder trucks, but Ozzie's job was to protect the show's money. And the crew. Late at night, as they were working on the tents, he'd show up suddenly with a garbage bag full of donuts and bagels—he'd stop by a Dunkin' Donuts just as they were closing and about to throw out their leftovers, and say, "Hey, can I get those? I have a circus to feed!"

Scratch a Smirko from Ozzie's era and you can get an endless number of stories. Like the time the sweltering bus was stuck in Boston traf-

fic on a hot day and Ozzie whipped out his bullhorn, leaned out the window and started yelling, "You crazy people, why do you live in this city??!!" while the troupers ducked, trying to hide from view.

But mostly, he was the tour dad. He would patrol the tables at mealtimes during training to make sure everyone was eating their vegetables. He was constantly reminding troupers to reuse things as much as possible. "He'd walk up to the water cooler and pull a crinkled piece of paper out, unfolding a pathetic, wrinkled cup that could barely hold water," remembers Francey Grund. Once a tour he would give the kids a lecture about junk food. "You know," he'd say, "some of the junk they put into sodas, the bags it comes in at the factories have a *skull and bones* on them. You're putting poison into your bodies!"

But he also seemed to know every waterfall, swimming hole and beautiful lake along the road in New England and, ferrying troupers from site to site, would stop along the way to let them cool down. Or he'd pull over to the side of the road and tell everyone to get out and look at the mountains. "Why?" they'd ask. "Just look at them and enjoy it!" he'd order.

One memorable day, he suddenly stopped the bus by a town square and had the troupers pile out: a church steeple was getting raised into place. "Be quiet and watch," he told them. "Nobody gets to see this these days."

"Well," says Sam Brown, "I don't know if you've ever watched a church steeple getting raised, but it does not take 10 minutes, as Ozzie promised." They sat there for four hours before moving on to the next tent site; it was their entertainment for the day. "Boy, were they grumpy when they got to the tent," remembers Troy.

And he had a keen eye for the kids who needed extra care and attention. Pat Mannion, who grew up in a tough town with a single mom, says, "Ozzie was my first positive male role model at Smirkus. He was the first to give me a noogie, the first ever to ask me about my home life, the first to be interested in whether Smirkus was something I'd do again. I never went home directly after Smirkus—I'd stay at Ozzie's house with him for a few days, and we'd fish on his lake."

These days, Ozzie's retired from Smirkus. Except that when he gets an emergency call to come fix a truck or help out with odd jobs around the Barn, he shows up right away. And somehow, he still gets to know each new lot of troupers. So when he says, "Smirkus? It was a hard ride, but it was a great ride," putting it in the past tense as if he's all done, you can't quite take him at his word.

Dear ozzie,
why should I want to come back.
for my whole summer I was
put to work cleaning toilets and pots.
and instead of us getting Paid We
pay You! I had to put on makeup
about 2 times a day, waike
up at 7:00 to exesise and train,
I had to put up with all
that B.S. from patrick,
getting yelled at by Valodia.
putting up a tent and taking it
down a 10:00 in the night
driving in a bus for
hours, Picking up other people garbege
under the seats.

OF COURSE I
WANT TO COME
BACK!!

From,
STEVIE The
Great!

CHAPTER SEVEN

LACE CANVAS POUND STAKES

Raising the Big Top

It was 2008 and Smirkus was performing in New York State for the first time. The tent had just gone up on the grounds of the historic Saratoga Springs horse-racing track when state Department of Labor inspectors arrived. The site inspector was new, only three weeks on the job. His boss had picked this day to ride with him and show him the ropes. They arrived three hours before show time and announced there would be no performance. "You don't have approval from the state engineer, and nothing happens without his stamp," they declared.

The state engineer had had the permit application for three months. Only now was Smirkus learning there was a problem. Ed LeClair, executive director and himself an engineer, got on the phone. The assigned engineer had received the required calculations for Smirkus's beautiful Italian designed-tent, but was having trouble understanding what they meant. All over the lot you could hear Ed screaming, "It's not Italian, you nitwit. It's metric!"

After an hour of frantic foot-to-metric conversions, Sara Wunderle miraculously found a sympathetic licensed architect who could verify the plans. Ed handed the phone to the on-site inspector.

"Uh huh," he said. "Tent approved? OK." He handed the phone back. "Your tent is approved, but I still have a problem with the bleachers." This was the first mention of the bleachers. It was 90 minutes until showtime. The inspector held his tape measure up to the small opening between the bleacher seats and the plate that narrows the gap with the floor. "This is six inches," he said. "Needs to be four. If a tiny baby was crawling around on the audience's feet, it could fall through. You can't use these bleachers in the State of New York."

The cast and crew huddled. Judy Gaeth, the circus operations director, calmly laid out the plan. "I need everybody on bleachers: cooks, counselors, cast, crew, concessions,

CIRCUS
SMIRKUS

everyone!" she said. "I want the bleachers down, out and safely stacked before I get back. Sara, you and I are going to go find 500 folding chairs. Troy, hit the midway and take care of the audience."

What happened next was a defining moment. Everyone on the lot pitched in, aware there was no Plan B. Working feverishly but in good spirits, with a line of audience members watching curiously, they unscrewed a thousand bolts, wing nuts and screws and carried five tons of aluminum bleachers out the two small side entrances.

With the bleachers gone the tent looked cavernous, but it made it easy to load in the 500 chairs Judy had found. As the last row went in, the crew crowded around Judy, who turned to the inspector triumphantly. "We set?" she asked.

The inspector shook his head. "Those seats aren't tied down. You've got to maintain a fire lane between rows. Each seat needs to be tied to the seat next to it." It got very quiet in the tent. Tent boss Nat Brown slipped out and returned a few minutes later with a jumbo-sized coil of rope and a fork lift loaded with four-foot iron Big Top stakes. "Those chairs aren't going anywhere," he smiled.

Sledgehammers flying, the tent crew drove the tent stakes into the end of each row of chairs and roped them all together. As the last stake was driven in, a cheer went up. The inspector nodded and handed Judy the permit. The doors opened—just 15 minutes late.

Epilogue: Annoyed by the state's approach to the whole affair, site presenter and trouper parent Robert Sanson dug into the regulatory code and discovered that the Department of Labor's requirements applied only to for-profit companies. Smirkus is a nonprofit, and should have been exempt from everything the inspectors had demanded. "Robert was like a dog on a blood scent," says Judy. These days, the circus sets up in Saratoga Springs with no problems.

What is most striking to an outsider watching a Smirkus show get put together and presented some 70 times during a summer is the unending hard work, bottomless dedication and sheer, bullheaded resilience displayed by the adults behind the scenes. About halfway through the tour his first year with Smirkus, Sonny Barringer, a ramrod of an ex-Marine who served on the crew for a few years in the late '90s, approached Ozzie Henchel.

"Sir," he asked, "how long have you been doing this?"

"Oh," Ozzie answered, "this'll be my seventh year."

"And you're not dead yet, sir?" Sonny replied.

The men and women who keep Smirkus running may not be standing in the lights when a full tent erupts in a standing ovation, but they bask in it every bit as fully as the troupers because they know what it took to get there. And what did it take? Here are a few glimpses...

COACHES

Over the years, Smirkus has pulled in coaches from every continent but Antarctica. Though their styles, ideas and even circus techniques are as varied as their backgrounds, they all have had the same goal: to take the raw material they're given and come up with an act that's enjoyable and artistically striking, that uses each performer's particular talents and that fits flawlessly into the show.

The challenge, of course, is doing all this in three weeks. And it's not just a matter of teaching technique and demonstrating an act's often intricate choreography. "We're also teaching them the process of putting together a group number, which is not about 'This is my best trick,'" says Bill Forchion, a former Ringling clown and Cirque du Soleil performer who coached *Smirkusology* and *Smirkus Ever After.* "It's about figuring out how to 'phrase' a piece and move it along so it crescendos in a way that's worthwhile to the audience."

Coaching at Smirkus is a constant improvisation. Not only must coaches assess how strong and skilled their performers are and how they can best be showcased, but also how capable they'll be of sustaining what's being asked of them over the course of an entire summer. They have to plunge deep into psychology—when the trapeze girl who's fine doing a toe hang at six feet in the air discovers she can't at eight feet or when the gifted tumbler who's done a double backflip off a teeterboard 50 times in a safety harness suddenly freezes when it's time for the lines to come off. They are literally the adults in the tent, so they have to make tough

Facing page: Judy Gaeth, **top**; tent boss Nat Brown with sledge, **bottom**.
This page (clockwise from top right): Troy and Sara Wunderle and coaches Genne Totukhov; Serenity Smith-Forchion and Elsie Smith; Jenny Ritchie, Alisan Funk, Estelle Borel; Chimgee Haltarhuu and Zina Avgustova; Bilgee Batmunkh and Sellam Ouahabi.

"One of the things that keeps me going is just how much I feel valued in this job. Or the e-mails we get: 'We were able for two hours to forget our troubles and dilemmas and just watch these kids.' It's not every day you can go somewhere like that and forget real life for a bit."

—Sara Wunderle,
assistant operations director

Willow's Blog

Former trouper Willow Yonika was head counselor for the 2011 tour; she wrote an occasional blog: "One of my favorite things about Smirkus that I often find myself smiling about is 'contrast.'

• Small performers getting along famously with burly, tattooed tent crew members.

• A trouper who can work out for 12 hours, stretched beyond human limits by a crazy Moroccan coach, and never complains, but bursts into tears after getting poked by accident.

• Troupers being more professional and responsible than imaginable for their age, and then running across pavement with broken glass on it in bare feet.

• Hanging upside down by their toes on a trapeze; being totally surprised when I allow them to climb a tree."

decisions about what stays in the show and what doesn't. Sometimes they'll spend three weeks training performers on a new apparatus with great promise, only to find at the end that the act didn't quite get to the point of being dependably injury-proof; so despite the weeks of work, it gets cut.

And then, of course, coaches aren't just coaches. They build props, weld apparatus, act as cheerleaders, critics and confidants—and do pretty much anything else the circus needs. "Most of the coaches go above and beyond, staying up to all hours building props, making costumes, sewing buttons on during dress rehearsal so the costumers can get other things done," says Elsie Smith, an aerials coach through both the Jeff & Julie and Troy & Jesse years. "When the radio says there's a storm coming, everyone runs around and ties stuff down—it doesn't matter who you are. In the modern traditional circus, everyone does everything, because it's the only way you can get by."

COUNSELORS

Their job is to help troupers navigate the demands of an intense summer—in short, making sure they're happy and healthy. As former trouper Josh Shack, who also served as head counselor for several years, puts it, "Instead of controlling them, we're there to help them make good choices: to be safe wearing shoes when the apparatus demands it, to not do a trick alone when no one is around to watch, to eat well and get enough sleep."

Smirkus has always tried to cultivate both self-reliance and a sense of communal responsibility, which makes the counselor's job an interesting balancing act. "Often," says former trouper and head counselor Rachel Schiffer, "it's the troupers who step in and lift someone up if needed. It's the head counselor's responsibility to foster that environment, to have high expectations of the troupe so they can be a cohesive, strong body."

OPERATIONS DIRECTORS

There's a reason that Sonny Barringer was amazed that seven years of Smirkus hadn't yet killed Ozzie: Ozzie was the tour manager. In the early days, when Smirkus was always short of funds, its trucks and buses were constantly breaking down; Ozzie knew every second-hand auto-parts supply store between Greensboro and Martha's Vineyard. Getting a couple dozen troupers, several dozen more crew, tents, bleachers, rigging, props, a cook bus—known as the "pie car"— and a small convoy of dodgy vehicles all over New England under intense time pressure was hard enough. Toss in broken equipment, the occasional misfit tent-crew member, sleepless nights and the ever-present threat of bad weather, and you understand why Sonny had valid concerns for Ozzie's health.

These days the vehicles are more reliable, but the job is no easier. It's held down by Judy Gaeth and her assistant, Sara Wunderle. "I feel a deep connection with the tour staff because I'm so appreciative of all the blood and guts they put into taking this tour down the

road," says Judy. "I recognize what it means to come through all these situations we get into every year and come out with a sense of accomplishment. We're such a tight group of people, we all have each other's backs; I don't know where else you can work where you can get that. We may not have all the answers, but we'll all be there together to take care of whatever messes come up and feel good about it at the end."

And as for those surly inspectors? "Well," says Judy, "they come in with a preconceived notion that the circus is a bunch of no-gooders. So we treat them with sugar and spice and yes-sirs and the utmost respect, and generally when they leave the lot they've become believers. Especially when they walk over the lot and see how beautifully it's done and what attention to detail we take with all we do."

Make Roll to These Pieces

Shouting encouragement during teardown is a time-honored Smirkus tradition. Tent crew, tech crew, concessions, musicians, everyone on the lot is working with controlled abandon to get the tent down and ready to roll. As the night gets later and later, cast and crew alike keep the energy high by shouting out support to each other over the clang of steel and thump of the teardown music. "Tent Crew Rocks!" and "Troupers Rule!" sound back and forth through the tent.

Over the years, some peculiar exhortations have become classics. Long ago one of the Russian coaches was urging the troupers to roll up the wrestling mats that lie under the ring curb so they could be loaded in the truck. "Make roll to these pieces!" he shouted, trying his best to participate. The troupe loved it. It caught on. Years after the actual event had been lost to history, the spirit captured by that statement—the spirit of everyone pitching in to get the job done—remains part of Smirkus culture. In fact it has taken on a life of its own. During the first teardown of the tour, new troupers have no idea what everyone is saying and a whole new series of expressions develop... "Make rolls to this pizza!" "Make room for these pieces!" "Make love to this pizza?" Finally the original story gets told and the bond between Smirkus history and the latest cast and crew starts growing all over again.

Dynamic Rigging

Cris Clark, one-time Smirko and now Smirkus's head rigger, created the system of "dynamic rigging" that allows a trapeze or lyra not just to swing, but to rise and fall during an act. Bigger circuses do this with motors that can cost $10,000 apiece. Cris uses people—harnessed to a polymer rope that's as strong as steel but flexible enough to pass through pulleys and tie off in knots. At any Smirkus show you're certain to see a few shadowy figures in climbing harnesses scampering up and down the four masts that hold up the tent, as performers in the ring swoop and glide from the ground to the top of the tent and back.

Flagging the Tent

You can climb a circus tent up its outside walls, clinging to the vertical seams and then making your way to the center, where you sit with what feels like a thousand feet of canvas below you. This is the tent crew's aerie, though in the old days a few senior troupers each year also earned the privilege of climbing up barefoot to attach the Smirkus banner between the two front poles, the last act of setup. Chris Butler, who was on the tent crew for much of the first half of Smirkus's life, knew why kids were so drawn to the climb. "The tent was part of all of us, as if it had its own heartbeat," he says. "You wanted to be up on top of it, watching the fog roll across the valley and the cars start to pull in, listening to kids playing and the music starting up, putting those flags on top that say 'Circus Smirkus' across them, lying up there watching the sun set, watching the people leave the show and get in their cars, their kids laughing and happy—the tent had a spirit and we all wanted to be part of it."

TENT CREW

It's a given of circus life that in any summer, you'll face one or two torrential rains. In 2007, the year of *The Zoot Suit Caper,* they never stopped. Mud got everywhere: clothes, hair, vehicles, equipment. Putting up and taking down a circus is kind of like performing a square dance, do-si-doing with heavy equipment and 20-pound sledgehammers. Add in mud day after day and it quickly loses its allure. "You can deal with one grueling setup or teardown," says Nat Brown, tent boss since 2007 and older brother of Smirko clown Sam Brown. "But when they're stacked up one after another? Site after site, the generator, the stake pounder... everything axle-deep in peanut-butter-brown muck. In order to get our equipment anywhere, we had to lay down a plywood highway. But Smirkus tent crew turned that year into a game: We're going to make it happen, so why be miserable while we do it?"

When the weather's good, it takes about four hours to get the tents down and the trucks loaded. When it's not, it can take all night.

Putting the tent up is more painstaking. First the tractor-trailer that carries it has to be centered on the spot where the tent will be centered; the crew then pounds in stakes and the stakes that hold the masts, and raises the masts by hand, inch by inch. They're leveled out, wired together and hooked up to the top of the tent, the cupola. That—along with the attached tent—then gets raised, also inch by inch, using a hand-cranked Tirfor winch. "We have to keep everything level; you can't just crank it up," says Nat. "You're moving thousands of pounds with every crank." Once the four large pieces of tent fabric are suspended safely in the air, the whole tent gets laced together from bottom to top, side poles get put in and as the tractor-trailer is driven out, the tent boss goes around the tent adjusting the tension on each of the straps that connect it to the ground—every site is different, depending on the minute geography of slopes and bumps. Setting up the tent, not counting the bleachers, rigging, lights and so on, takes about four hours, an astoundingly short time.

"I work at other circuses the rest of the year," says Nat, "and I miss Smirkus, because it's such an effortless thing. Everyone knows what they're doing and they're proud of what they do, whereas at other circuses I'm holding people's hands all the way through."

Of course, the crew's not done yet. There are the concessions tents to set up, and the backstage dressing/makeup tent. The various trailers have to be put in place, water lines hooked up, the washer and dryer connected (they'll be used for cleaning costumes), the dishwashing station put up. But in relatively short order, an entire small community is up and running where none existed just a few hours before. And in two or three days, they'll take it all down, haul it to the next town and put it up again.

COOK

Imagine a buffet line of 30 hungry teenagers. Some have the appetite of starving wolverines, others mull each choice as if it's the only thing they'll eat that day. In line with them are 30 to 60 adults eager to be refueled for another workday and excited to see what culinary treats have been prepared to distract them from the sameness of life on the road. It's your job to cook for them in a space that makes the average studio apartment's kitchen look palatial. Welcome to the pie car.

On a crew of people who work exceptionally hard, the cooks may work the hardest. They're at the stovetop every morning by 5:30, getting breakfast ready. There might be a short break before they have to start preparing lunch, but often there isn't. There are afternoon snacks to get out, then dinner, then evening snacks, and then the pie car has to be prepped for breakfast. They usually finish between 8 and 9 p.m., unless it's a teardown night, in which case they're dishing out sandwiches to the crew until early in the morning. Amazingly, they create these nutritious, calorie-dense meals for 60 (on tour) to 90 (during training) people from a couple of stockpots, two skillets and a few pans. "You have to get really creative and use your equipment in ways that it's not really meant to be used," says Katie Schroeder, who joined Smirkus in 2010 as cook and took over as head cook in 2011.

Which is exactly what appeals to Katie. "Every day in the pie car is like your mom's kitchen on steroids," she says. "You have the total freedom within the kitchen to create whatever you see fit that day. You can play with things and have fun and let the creative juices run wild."

Despite the summer-long challenges, the pie car turns out three excellent, varied meals a day, keeping vegan and carnivore alike happy and the finicky and voracious both well-fed. "If I'm having a really rough day and am at my wits' end, going down to the Big Top and watching a couple of acts gives me a huge boost," Katie says. "It helps me realize there's a reason I'm doing this and it's why I'm here, and that I wouldn't want to be anywhere else. I'd do anything just to be a part of this."

Above: Head cook Katie Schroeder in the Pie Car

"You're living with 60 people seven days a week, and three times a day you stop everything and have a meal with them. You really break your back working with them—in the sun, the mud, the rain, every day of the week—and then someone rings the bell and it's time to stop and have a meal together. If I were ever to do another tour, that's what I would be looking forward to."

—Peter Bufano, composer

BACKYARD, FRONT YARD

Even at a show, when Smirkus is at its most visible, you get only a hint of everything going on around you. You get your tickets from the "box office"—where Sara Wunderle and a crew of volunteers juggle hundreds of reservations, last-minute sales and names on the waiting list. Next you head for the tent, between concession stalls hawking cotton candy, clown noses, light wands, juggling balls and T-shirts, staffed by a crew who travel with the circus all summer. You hand your tickets to the volunteers standing by the entranceway, file through a dimly lit foyer lined with gaudily painted, mysterious posters—and pass under the tech booth, where the sound and lighting crew will spend the next two hours creating the magical array of moods that transport you to the land of suspended disbelief.

And once you're in your seat, you may or may not notice two other people critical to the show. But they are there, beyond the glare of the limelight.

It's the house manager's job to make sure that everything on the audience side of the ring curb stays on an even keel—which isn't always easy. The final day of the 2011 tour, just about the middle of the first act, the skies over Greensboro opened and it hailed—large, marble-size hail that caromed off the tent, found its way into the cupola and splashed on the lights, and built quickly into slushy piles on the tent-site grounds. Inside, the noise was deafening—so loud that the performers couldn't hear the music. The challenge was to keep the audience in the tent calm. "The troupers were amazing," says Brita Larson, who was house manager for the tour. "They kept in rhythm even when they couldn't hear the music; and because they stayed calm and composed, we could keep the audience calm and composed. Outside, the crew and troupers' parents were digging trenches and laying down plywood bridges. The audience didn't even realize everything that was going on. And that's how it was supposed to be."

Meanwhile, back behind the curtain, the production manager is making sure the show stays on track, working with the technicians, the rigger and the wardrobe mistress, checking on props, chasing down troupers who've forgotten their cues—and taking notes on everything that could be improved. Yet as demanding as all that may be, says Josh Shack, who these days is Smirkus's production manager, the hardest part of the job actually ends once the show hits the road. "No one does what we do in the amount of time we do it in, because it's insane," he says. "Most shows with our level of theatricality, original music, costuming and choreography hire existing acts and then put the rest together for six weeks or more. We do it in three. The fact that, as Troy says, we shouldn't be able to do this and yet do it every year, is testament to the magic of Smirkus."

Another Fine Mess

IT'S 2008. ALREADY ON THIS TOUR, Troy has driven a stake through a town water line. The pie car has come unhitched and passed the truck that was pulling it—on the Interstate. A new rental generator has fried all the lights in the tent.

Now the company arrives in Kennebunkport, Maine. The rain has been Biblical. Maneuvering the trucks just to get the site arranged takes hours of extra work. And then, as two days of rain-drenched shows unfurl, the trucks slowly start to sink. By the time the last spectator leaves the last show, the trucks are up to their axles in mud. The company is due in Montpelier the next morning.

Getting the tent and bleachers down and loaded turns out to be the easy part. Directed by Troy, who has a head for extricating big trucks from a cramped lot, the crew starts slamming four-foot tent stakes in front of the first truck, attaches one end of an industrial-strength come-along to the stakes and the other to the truck, lays down a bed of plywood and starts inching the truck out. They pull the stakes out, move them a few dozen feet, lay down more plywood and repeat, until finally the truck can be driven onto the roadway. That's just the first vehicle. There are 20 to go.

Daybreak finds them still at it, with four trucks still stuck. At which point Judy calls in the biggest wrecker she can find. Its driver doesn't even *try* to get his truck into the field—he just stands by the side of the road and throws the winch out to be hooked onto each truck. Once everything is finally out, the field is barren, with slabs of plywood sticking into the air every which way, like a vandalized cemetery. The crew, looking more clay than human, can barely move. Judy calls Rob, as she does about once a year, to ask, "What were you *thinking* when you started Smirkus?"

When the crew finally does pull into Montpelier, the tent trailer is already parked on the site. Across it is strung a clothesline hung with 20 pairs of fresh white socks and a message from Rob:

"There was lots of joy in Mudville...

"Back in the Old Blue days, the tent crew mutinied—they were tired and fed up over whatever it is that tent crews periodically get fed up about. They presented me and Ozzie

grab full buckets from the brigade and splash it over performers about to enter the ring: better soaked and clean than soaked and muddy.

"Backstage was shin-deep in mud and still the water poured down. The electric power was out, the ring was a wading pool and the brave little audience sat in raincoats waiting to see what would happen next, somehow creating the feeling that we were all in this together and they were playing their parts.

"Out came the ringmaster to announce: 'Ladies and Gentlemen! Welcome to Circus Smirkus...the MUD Show!!' The troupers ran out to happy cheers, five of them carrying fire torches and standing around the ring curb. I carried Molly on my shoulders into the ring and right onto the tightwire, as she danced barefoot on the wire holding an umbrella.

"This wasn't some dry indoor theater, this was circus! This was dirty, wet and passionate! This was the Killington Mountain Flash Flood, and everyone was having a blast. What choice was there?

"Then the show was over, the enthusiastic audience gone after a wet standing ovation, and the struggle to move trucks stuck in the mud began. Ozzie looked at me and shook his head, speaking the immortal words of Laurel & Hardy that I would hear from him a hundred times over the years: 'ANOTHER fine mess you've got me into, Mermin!'"

with a list of 10 demands that they wanted met before they'd agree to tear down the tent. Near the top was a demand for 'clean socks.' Remembering how strongly tent crews seem to feel about socks, I thought some nice, clean ones were the least I could do after the muddy yet heroic mess of Kennebunkport."

If you're going to live the vagabond circus life, then you've got to be ready for whatever it throws at you. "At all costs," says former trouper Dan Brown, "you just want to do the show the best you possibly can—the full show, too, not an abbreviated version." The lights go out? The jugglers have their fire torches prepped backstage and ready to go. The sound's gone? The troupers run for the ukulele and accordion. The show always manages to move on down the road. But you can always count on some kind of weather....

"Our second season, 1988," says Rob, *" we were given a site at the bottom of a mountainside in a dirt parking lot—every circus's worst scenario. One hour before showtime we watched the black clouds blow in over the mountain and hold a thunderous revival meeting over our little tent. The torrent of water cascaded down the mountainside right into the circus tent. In minutes the parking lot had turned to slick brown mud and the high wet winds battered the trucks, the tents...and the paying public!*

"There were 50 determined spectators shivering in the tent. They wouldn't leave, so we were equally determined to give them a show they would remember. The ring filled with two inches of water. Costumes got soaked. Tent crew ran around tightening guy ropes, pounding loose stakes deeper into the soft mud. The troupers, faces flushed with excitement, wore garbage bags over their costumes and tried desperately to cover wet props. I could read it in their faces: this was the life!

"Jade, 14 years old, instinctively took over as trench crew boss, shovel in hand. Molly, 12, ran to cover up her tightwire rigging. Doug, carrying a clown prop, slipped and belly-flopped in the mud, bravely holding the prop over his head. Porter bailed water from the ring. Toby led the bucket brigade, placing pails under the back door to collect rivulets coming off the tent. Duane stood by the back door to

Live Music at Smirkus!

Music propels circus. It brightens the tent, captures the exhilaration of a swinging trapeze, punctuates the pratfalls, inspires tears, gives extra spring to the acrobats. Without music, a circus is only half itself.

So from the very beginning, Smirkus has paid close attention to how it sounded. Its first three years, when he could barely scrape enough together to costume the troupers at Kmart, Rob hired musician Peter Tavalin to lead a live band with original music. "I was determined," he explains, "to create a traditional circus environment from the onset." Still, this was expensive, so he eventually turned to recordings. "That meant spending long hours late into the night using scissors and Scotch tape to splice together bits and pieces to fit the acts as they were developing in rehearsals," he remembers.

This began to change in 1999, when Rob hired Vermont folk musicians Colin McCaffrey and Pete Sutherland to write the soundtrack for *Robin Hood.* They produced a classic—original Celtic airs and dances from the British Isles—but it was still on a CD.

The next step in Smirkus's musical evolution came in 2002, with the *Wild West* show. Rob had decided it was time to reintroduce live music, and advertised in college publications for a bluegrass band. A group of sophomores at Middlebury College, the Route 7 Ramblers, noticed the ad and signed up. "We were delighted," remembers Caleb Elder, one of the band's leaders, "because it was a good story to tell and it was a funny thing to do for the summer."

Smirkus was hooked. Live music made the shows more exciting, giving them a sparkle that didn't come through with tape. The Ramblers came back for 2003, but then they graduated. Jeff and Julie Jenkins—who by now were directing—needed to find someone new.

In New York City early that year, they ran into Peter Bufano, who'd been at Clown College with Jeff and then abandoned clowning to compose circus music. In short order, Peter found himself writing the music for *Alice in Wonderland*, performing it with his four-piece Cirkestra... and learning that at Smirkus, a composer's life required its own sort of musical acrobatics.

"I'm writing the music for the juggling act and I want it to sound like this," Peter explains, "and the juggling act gets cut, but 'Oh, it would work out perfectly for the trapeze act.' So you take a song and change the length or the tempo so that it matches the trapeze act. I spent a lot of time walking around the circus barn, walking through the trees and writing in my imagination and not on a keyboard in the office. I was in the midst of it because I figured that's where people hear it."

In 2005, for *Pinocchio*, and again in 2007, for The *Zoot Suit Caper,* Peter and Cirkestra supplied the music. These jazzy, klezmer-inflected scores, with their growling horns, soaring violin, lonely accordion and kaleidoscopic shifts from sweet innocence to peppery mischief, defined Smirkus's sound throughout the mid-2000s.

In 2008, Tristan Moore signed on as the house composer. He 'd been drawn to Smirkus years before, after stumbling on *The Voyage of the Pirate Queen* in Stowe. "I sat in the audience marveling that something like this was possible in the U.S.," he recalls, "and thinking that maybe the circus in

Facing page: Peter Bufano
This page (clockwise from top left):
Peter Bufano; Tristan Moore; The Original Smirko Band, 1987; Route 7 Ramblers, 2002; Route 7 Ramblers, 2003

this country wasn't doing so badly after all. It was funny, daring, poetic, beautifully directed—and it felt like something I could see myself becoming part of." Eight years later, he did.

"One of the first things Troy, Jesse and I talk about, even before we talk about the acts, is giving each show its own unique sensibility," Tristan says. "We do themes partly as a way of guaranteeing that each year's show will be different from the last, but a convenient side effect for us as artists is that it keeps the process new and unpredictable. It helps keep us inspired and moving forward as artists." It also allows him to explore the music and movies and other cultural references that relate to the time period of that particular show. "It's a unique experience to be looking at history through the lens of music that defines the mood."

Circus music, he agrees, has to be flexible. "You have to build in stalling devices, repeats or infinitely expandable sections, so that you can follow the performers. The illusion for the audience is that the performers are following the music, but for Smirkus, the music is actually following the performers. So I'll approximate how long each section is going to be and build about that much music, and then will build an extension section that keeps the music going, and then an escalation for when, say, the jugglers hit a trick. It tells the audience that we've just hit that level of difficulty and now we're about to move up to the next level. The reward of doing the job right is the audience doesn't know it, they just feel it."

CHAPTER EIGHT

SMIRKUS® FOR ALL

Big Top Tour,
Smirkus Camps &
Ringmaster Residencies

People always expect me to use circus metaphors, but personally I think Smirkus is like watching a child grow. On the one hand it's the most ordinary thing in the world; on the other, it's a miracle.

—Ed LeClair, Executive Director

Smirkus "World Headquarters" operates out of "the Barn," a 135-year-old unadorned farmhouse with bare wooden floors and offices crammed into the original bedrooms, pantries and kitchens. Office furniture is hand-me-downs and cast-offs. The Executive Conference Room is still the kitchen table.

But as the silver anniversary arrives, it is an "operation" now, the collective dream of 25 years of cast and crew. It employs 10 year-round staff, including its executive, marketing and circus operations directors, an office manager, administrative staff and publicity specialist. It keeps artists busy all winter doing school residencies. During the summer it grows almost sevenfold, taking 45 people

on the road—everyone from tent crew to musicians to concessionaires—and hires some 32 coaches and counselors for Circus Smirkus Camp. The tour budget alone broke the million-dollar level long ago. The camp, which over the years has jumped from rented location to rented location around Vermont's Northeast Kingdom, has grown so large and successful that it needs its own site.

For 25 years the three programs—the Big Top Tour, Smirkus Camp and Ringmaster Residencies—have inspired kids and helped adults feel young at heart again. The managers and administrators have always been like riggers, keeping everything safe and operating smoothly so that the troupers, campers, backstage crew and counselors can put on their best act.

THE TOUR

Circus Smirkus is a nonprofit, and from the beginning part of its mission has been to help other nonprofit organizations. During the winter the operations director—first Ozzie Henchel, now Judy Gaeth—gets in touch with nonprofit organizations throughout New England, from town recreation departments to children's museums to private schools, to ask if they want to present Smirkus in their town. For many of these groups, Smirkus represents the major fundraising event of the year; Smirkus helps with marketing, while the groups organize homestays, sell tickets and promote the show locally. They pay a contract fee to Smirkus, and then keep all ticket sales to generate profits for their group. Over the years, Smirkus has helped its presenting partners raise $2.4 million.

The most important trick to success, though, is for Smirkus to build a relationship with the communities it visits. Local businesses get involved with sponsorships, local groups arrange circus dinners and workshops and Smirkus gives backstage tours to kids in need, making the circus a community-wide event. And Smirkus has developed strong ties over the years to organizations like the Barbara Bush Children's Hospital in Portland, Maine, where troupers

An Express Mission

As a 501c3 nonprofit organization, Circus Smirkus has an express mission: To promote the skills, culture and traditions of the traveling circus and to inspire youth to engage in life-enhancing adventures in the circus arts.

put on a show every year, and to a variety of Waldorf schools around New England, which enthusiastically present Smirkus and take advantage of its presence for workshops.

FRIENDS FOREVER

Sometimes, Smirkus's impact on a community and a family—and the family's and community's impact on Smirkus—can last long after the tent crew pulls up stakes and moves on down the road for the last time.

For two years, Smirkus traveled to Simsbury, Connecticut, after Betsy and Niels van Gemeren saw it in New Hampshire and convinced their local private school, the Cobb School, to present it. The van Gemerens and their three children put troupers up during those years, and when Troy Wunderle returned to town to do residencies at Cobb, he stayed with them. He taught the kids to juggle, took them on long unicycle rides and grew especially close to their son, Willem, an effervescent boy who became, in Troy's words, "like a long-distance little brother."

In 2005, Niels and Willem were killed as they were returning from a visit to Betsy's brother; their small airplane crashed just after takeoff. Willem was 11. Smirkus was performing on Cape Cod, and when Troy heard the news he drove to Simsbury so he could see Betsy and the girls and offer them a hug, then turned around and drove back to the tour site.

Willem's friends at the Cobb School, where he was a popular baseball player, decided they needed to do something in his honor. They set up a group at school, Friends Forever, which holds a fundraising picnic every year called Willem's Field of Dreams; the proceeds go to Smirkus and to the humane society in North Conway, New Hampshire, where Willem got his cat.

There are very few kids left at the school who knew Willem, yet the ties to Smirkus endure. Troy still visits for residencies. Cobb School families send their children to Smirkus Camp and drop by shows throughout the summer, to cheer the troupers on and say hello. Betsy's family helped rescue Smirkus after its financial troubles in 2005. And the last year Smirkus was in North Conway, Betsy hosted the entire troupe for a homestay at her parents' house—"Smirkus is such an incredible entity," she says, "that anybody who can experience it, at any level, is lucky to be involved."

If you happen to catch a Smirkus show, look for a gorilla near the entrance as you walk in. That was a gift from the van Gemerens too. It was Willem's.

RESIDENCIES

Working with kids in schools is a natural for Smirkus. Since its inception, the Ringmaster Residency program has been one of Smirkus's best avenues for showing kids and their parents the joys of learning circus skills. Some 40 times a year, Smirkus's residency artists take over a school for a day, a week or even two weeks. They will work with teachers to weave circus into the everyday curriculum and work with students—as many as 500 or more at a time—to learn circus skills and finish up the week with a show.

It is both satisfying and demanding work. "As a residency artist you need to be good at everything," says Troy Wunderle, who joined Rob as a young clown in doing residencies and took over the job shortly after. "You have to have a genuine interest, love and respect for children. You have to be a very good entertainer. You have to be a director and producer and understand how to put a show together with the talents that the kids both do and don't have. You need to work well with the different personalities. Without hesitation I would tell you it's harder to create a good residency show than a good Smirkus show!"

Maybe the best way to understand the residency program is through this story from Rick Davis, a longtime circus educator, who now runs the Ringmaster Residencies.

Her arms never pointed in the same direction. Her eyes were fixed downward. Her body was bent. Cerebral palsy is cruel and Annie did not deserve it, but it was hers for life.

It was show day on the final day of a school residency and the students had chosen the acts they wished to perform. Easy for most students, not so easy for Annie. Most assumed she could not participate. Time came for the globe-balancing act and students lined up to take their turns standing tall on the big, intimidating ball. I had expected six students but there, to my surprise, was a seventh at the end of the line: Annie.

As each student before her performed, you could feel the unspoken thoughts of the audience:

"Annie?"

"I loved it when you taught us the juggling. I tried it at home, but all I did was break some eggs and get yelled at. Please come back."

—Will S., Fourth Grade

"Standing on the globe?"

"Can she do it?"

I, too, was worried.

In my school residencies, I don't teach circus tricks, I teach circus "goals." I point students toward the tools they can use to reach their goals: TRY, TRY AGAIN, TRY A NEW WAY, WATCH, LISTEN, STEP-BY-STEP, GO SLOW, READ. I call these "Circus Secrets," and I ask students to use these tools whenever they hear a voice inside saying, "I can't do it." Annie must have taken these secrets to heart, because, with her eyes fixed on the globe, she was determined to try. I held her arms as she ascended. Her body shook as she sought balance. My knees braced the ball firmly so that Annie could find it. She was determined, and her determination inspired me to forget about keeping up the pace of the show, and to stay with her as long as it took. In globe balancing there is a precise moment when you know you have found your center, and everyone has a center, even if you have a body that is bent. The magic moment came to Annie. She at last found her center, realized her balance and started to rise a little taller, breathe a little calmer and smile with a brightness that pierced the audience's heart. I let go of her arms and Annie stood by herself. The crowd erupted.

Each of us can be more than we think we are. This is the message of circus. Humans are capable of incredible feats, and that goes for all of us, no matter who we are. For each of us there are feats that seem out of our reach. Some never even try. But during that school residency show, Annie showed us all that anyone can go further.

THE MORE THINGS CHANGE—BY ED LECLAIR

In 1989 a young solo clown bribed his way into Russia to meet with Alla Youdina and the Moscow Circus community. In Cuba 22 years later, directors Jesse Dryden and Troy Wunderle, coach Alisan Funk and I were greeted with full VIP treatment by the directors of Circuba, the national circus of Cuba, and Escuela Nacional de Circo, Cuba's national high school circus program.

Circuba had invited Smirkus to Havana to teach their performers about "contemporary circus." Our workshops were held in a magnificent old theater, gutted of all furnishings to make room for circus equipment. There was no electricity; light and ventilation had been provided by beating holes in the walls with sledgehammers. But the space was a metal maze of flying trapeze rigs, Russian swings and rigging cables, requiring a combination of high hurdles and the limbo to move around. Aerial choreographer Alisan Funk had been given a tiny space in the middle to conduct a workshop for 30 professional aerialists and kids from the school.

Meanwhile, in a balcony upstairs Troy and Jesse were surrounded by clowns. Birthday-party clowns, street-performing clowns, puppeteers, circus clowns and, a new one on me, aquarium clowns. Turns out that in Cuba, clowns have a union. And Local 491 was well represented. Forty-five of Havana's funniest were there, waiting for new material.

As the day wore on, Alisan struggled with difficult conditions and skepticism that a

North American could teach circus to Cubans. Troy and Jesse found that their translator had more opinions about humor than they did. They would provide a sentence of instruction and then listen to paragraphs of translation. All in all, it was a (circus) train wreck.

Over dinner we huddled, and in Smirkus style, regrouped. The next morning we moved Alisan upstairs and combined the groups. We moved the clowns onto trapeze and the aerialists into clowning. We recruited a drummer to give the room some juice. With rhythms echoing off the walls, the mood became playful. Jesse urged the group into constantly changing improvisational acts. The Smirkus coaches shouted instructions amidst people laughing, dancing and chasing each other. Everyone seemed reconnected to the original spirit of why people do circus in the first place.

An audience gathered. The professionals working out downstairs stopped by to watch. The coaches from Escuela showed up. When we broke for lunch there was applause and groans of disappointment that we were stopping.

The euphoria continued for two more days. Alisan developed several aerial acts and Jesse and Troy crafted a *charivari*, finale and numerous clown entrees. All was going famously as we prepared for our final presentation performance in the main Circuba big top.

The opening flowed seamlessly and the *charivari* had the entire tent clapping and stomping their feet. A Cuban coach leaned over and commented, "All this in three days?"

The wheels fell off with the second act. The music was all wrong. The clowns abandoned the gags they'd developed with Troy and Jesse to perform their own material. The tech staff was experienced enough to know that the music they were playing could not be right, so they just kept pushing buttons until they found something they liked.

But in Cuba, such situations are expected, and they loved that in universal circus fashion we responded with "the show must go on." After a series of painful clown entrees, Alisan's group aerial acts shone through the mistimed light fades and rapidly changing music. Her graceful gang aerial-dance competition—think the Montagues vs. the Capulets to a salsa beat—set the stage for a high-energy finale. The crowd roared its approval.

Backstage the coaches and directors of the Cuban circuses shook our hands and pounded our backs. I was ushered into a small room with the Cuban circus hierarchy. They broke out the rum and proceeded to outline our future exchange rules. "Every year, Smirkus comes and teaches us. We send you young coaches and kids, you teach them too. If you want, we can make a show here in Cuba and send it anywhere you like." Mission accomplished.

The idea that I explore Cuba as a source of coaches and talent had originally come from Rob. Standing backstage in Havana I thought about him, his connection to Russia, Cuba's connection to Russia and how some giant circle, some enormous circus ring was being completed through a small mud show in Greensboro. Hup Hey, Smirkos! Start working on your Spanish.

Above: Executive Director Ed LeClair arriving at the office

DEAR PARENTS

From a fundraising letter Ed LeClair sent to the parents of troupers:

Every year Smirkus takes a cast photo. Thirty young faces, all smiles and swagger. Expressions somewhere between fawns in the headlights and "let me at 'em." You probably still have one hanging on a wall. It's covered with inside jokes and promises of friendship eternal.

Look closer. I think maybe I see something you don't. There behind the kids, just out of the photographer's frame. It's the back story. I see the parents who in many ways had their own loosely held but fondly treasured cast. I can see your first-year hesitancy and blossoming pride. I remember your guilty pleasure of sneaking away from your volunteer post to watch the opening charivari, and the slow, incredulous smile creeping onto your face as your trouper burst through the curtain for the first time. In later years, I see you oh-so-kindly taking other starstruck mothers and fathers under your wing to let them know: "It's gonna be OK. Your kid is going to be safe, sound and deliriously happy. Sit back, relax and enjoy the show."

This is the story at Smirkus that seldom gets told. The story of the elephant-sized effort that the parents all give to make this place work. You give money, you give time, you give rides and homestays and brownies and then more money and ultimately something only you can bestow. You give your blessing. You say yes. You let them run away and do something absolutely crazy that many people won't understand, and you say to your child, "I bless it, because it makes you happy."

MIRKUS

CIRCUS SMIRKUS® CAMP

Early on, Rob realized that demand for running away to the circus far exceeded the limits of one small ring. In 1991 he started Smirkus Camp to serve the crowds of kids knocking on the tent door. Through the mid-'90s, Circus Smirkus Camp consisted of a couple of two-week sessions with about 40 kids at each. Today, 420 young people from ages 5 to 18 go to any of seven different camp sessions, from a one-day "Smirkling Camp" to a two-week, intensive circus Advanced Camp for older kids who are serious about their training. Even with all that, there's a waiting list to get in.

Its allure is that Smirkus Camp works hard to maintain a delicate balance between being a focused circus-arts training facility and providing kids with a fun and exciting adventure. "When kids first see the tents, their jaws drop and their eyes start to sparkle," says Mary Blouin Auffert, who ran the camp for nine years. "The dream has come true and they are about to step right up and live it." And there are fun camp traditions, like costumed dinners and Pie Day, when kids learn not only how to make soap pies, but to throw them at each other, the staff and—if parents happen to be visiting—their parents. Of course, in fair play the parents also get to pie their kid.

Many of the kids, though not all of them, arrive with the secret dream of becoming a star performer. In the one or two weeks camp staff have to work with them, that's a tall order. Still, Advanced Camp offers the chance—kids can focus on a particular act and polish both their technique and their performance skills, or they can join "Road Show," which puts a show together and then takes it to nursing homes, day-care centers and other venues.

Even so, says Mary, "The basic point of camp is not to make performers out of them in one week or to get highly skilled kids

that we then choose from and move along, but to help every single kid have a wonderful time learning circus skills and to become a circus lover for life."

Along the way, of course, any number of kids also learn the skills, confidence and performance smarts to go on tour or put themselves on a professional track, but a lot of kids are happy just to stay immersed in camp. The same lessons in understanding, tolerance and feeling free to be oneself that kids find on the Smirkus tour, they also find at camp—it's where, no matter who you are, you fit in. "No one's going to judge them," says Megan Rose, who along with Jessica Labun took over running the camp from Mary in 2007. "They can try things out they wouldn't get to do at home, and no one's going to pick on them for it."

In fact, Megan and Jessica are the perfect examples of

Smirkus Camp's influence. You might think of them as "The Campers Who Stayed."

Megan got to Smirkus Camp at age 16, a year too old at the time to be a camper, but just old enough to be a counselor. Intensely shy, she didn't talk her first week. The camp director pulled her aside eventually and asked, "Do you want to be here?" She did. She began taking classes along with the campers, especially former Ringling clown Ted Lawrence's lessons in clowning. "That's when I started feeling comfortable and realized it was OK to open up," she remembers. "It helped me step into conversations that I wouldn't normally have stepped into, because what was the worst thing that could happen to you? Someone might laugh. Big deal. Smirkus makes you feel safe and try out things that you might not do anywhere else." Megan had found a home.

One of her strongest memories from that first summer was how impressed she was by one of the girls crossing a tightwire with a boy on her shoulders. The girl was Jessica Labun.

Jessica started at Smirkus Camp when she was eight—you had to be nine to go, but her father lied on the application. When one of the counselors asked her how old she was, she broke down. "I'm eight!" she cried. "I'm eight! Please don't send me home!" They didn't.

Though a gymnast, she was drawn immediately to the tightwire. Her coach was Jade Kindar-Martin,

> In fact, Megan and Jessica are the perfect examples of Smirkus Camp's influence. You might think of them as "The Campers Who Stayed."

and in the final show that year, when Jade lay down on the wire, it was Jessica who got to cross, step on his chest, and keep going. "That," she says, "was the coolest thing ever!"

As the years went on, what kept her coming back was that, just like Megan, she'd found a home away from home. "I wasn't especially popular at school," she says, "and camp was where I found a place and a community. It was a place where I could be myself, do cool and interesting things that I didn't get to do anywhere else in the world and meet amazing people from places like Moscow and Mongolia. All I know is, none of my other friends were having that experience!"

A Smirkus Camp Flapjack

Rob Mermin: One of the most touching philanthropic donations Smirkus ever received came from a young Vermonter, Kyle M. When he was four, he started sending Smirkus one-third of his chore allowance—$1.33 in change—to put into a fund so he could attend camp when he grew up. That was his dream, and for years, the office received his faithfully mailed letter, with the money, a picture and a note... "With love." Eventually, Kyle became a camper.

Years later, rummaging through some old letters, I came across the first one Kyle had sent. I brought it to give to Kyle's father, who owned the local diner. Kyle's dad sat down, read the letter, and with wet eyes pointed to the date—in Kyle's childish handwriting, there was that day's date, 15 years earlier. Unaware, I had come to deliver the letter on the anniversary of Kyle's first down payment. Kyle himself, now a cook, was flipping pancakes behind the counter. In honor of the occasion, he made me an oversized clown pancake with raisins for eyes, a cherry nose and a whipped-cream mouth: a Smirkus Camp Flapjack.

Above, **at right**, Mary Blouin Auffert, former camp director; **right**, camp staff, 2001

"There was this one show for Advanced Camp—I was busy doing costumes and never got to see rehearsals. Finally, when they were doing the "stumble-through" I decided the kids had to see me at a rehearsal. My jaw dropped. The premise was that a ship gets wrecked on an island, and at the very beginning of the show, the kids rolled in as waves; then the waves got bigger and bigger, and they became this two-high ship with masts and sails that moved so fluidly and gracefully, rocking as it sailed. A storm blew in, the ship wrecked, fell apart, and the kids became waves again. I wept, it was so beautiful."

—Mary Blouin Auffert

Highlights in the Limelight!

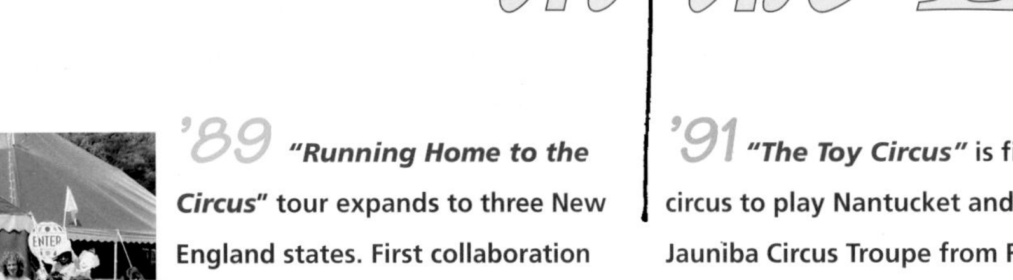

'87 Rob Mermin creates Circus Smirkus in old farmhouse in Vermont's Northeast Kingdom. Northern VT Tour: one whole week! "First Vermont-based circus in over 100 years." (*Boston Globe*) Media coverage in *The New York Times.* Vermont cows bemused by all the commotion.

'88 ***"Vermont's Own Homegrown Country Circus"*** hits the road with 28 shows, 11 towns, 3 weeks. Coverage in *USA Today*. With Smirkus coaches, Rob produces end-of-summer fair circus for the next dozen years with a state fair in CT. Two week "Circus Residency" in New England schools initiated. Vermont teachers bemused by all the commotion.

'89 ***"Running Home to the Circus"*** tour expands to three New England states. First collaboration with Project Harmony; guest troupe from Tbilisi, Georgia, USSR. Articles in *Yankee* and *People* magazines. Freak tornado hits Putney, VT: trees and telephone poles down, but Old Blue stands alone and the show goes on by torchlight.

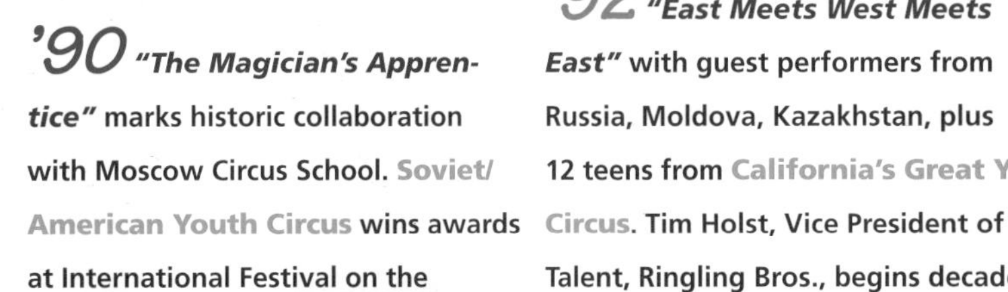

'90 ***"The Magician's Apprentice"*** marks historic collaboration with Moscow Circus School. Soviet/American Youth Circus wins awards at International Festival on the

Black Sea. Performances in Yaroslavl, Moscow and Vermont. Dubbed "The Vodka and Maple Syrup Tour." Smirkus summer camp opens to boisterous laughter and rowdy antics of little children. Parents are bemused.

'91 ***"The Toy Circus"*** is first circus to play Nantucket and includes Jauniba Circus Troupe from Riga, Latvia. Soviet/American Youth Circus-On-Ice with Rob and Alla on skates plays Vermont in winter. Soviet coup leaves Russians and Latvians stranded at the barn. Emotions run high. Cows worried.

'92 ***"East Meets West Meets East"*** with guest performers from Russia, Moldova, Kazakhstan, plus 12 teens from California's Great Y Circus. Tim Holst, Vice President of Talent, Ringling Bros., begins decade of annual scouting visits. He is seen contentedly mowing the lawn at Smirkus headquarters and talking to the cows. Smirkus receives Vermont Arts Council Award of Excellence. If they only knew what really goes on…

'93 ***"The Princess Who Wouldn't Laugh"*** is Smirkus's first "story circus" and features classical music, Russian artists and 10 First Nation Indian performers in collaboration with Ringling Bros. Vermont Chamber names Smirkus a *"Top Ten Summer Event."* Cover story in the *Boston Globe* Sunday Magazine. Indians astonish everyone one day: dancing seriously in full regalia, feathered headdresses—and Groucho Marx glasses.

'94 ***"Houdini Lives"*** escapes with artists from Russia and Mongolia and Smirkos from around the USA. Smirkus featured in *The Chronicle of Philanthropy.* ***FamilyFun*** magazine rates Smirkus as one of *"America's Best Circuses."* Actor Michael J. Fox visits the tour. Smirkus video receives Dove Foundation Award for Family Values. Acts showcase straightjacket escapes in midair, trick handcuff stunts, metamorphosis trunks, disappearances, levitations and magical transformations: things every kid should know but never learns in school.

'95 ***"Class Clowns"*** has guest performers from Russia, Mongolia, Hungary, and first cultural exchange with Budapest Circus School.

Founder Rob Mermin appointed Dean of Ringling Bros. and Barnum & Bailey Clown College. Two Smirkos graduate from Clown College and win contracts with Ringling, opening the doors for a dozen future Smirkus/Ringling clown connections.

'96 ***"Lights, Action, Circus!"*** portrays a 1920s Hollywood camera crew, the whole audience as extras. Smirkus again named *"Top Ten Summer Event."* Trouper graduates go pro with Ringling, Cirque du Soleil and European circuses. First Smirko Rhodes Scholar. Playwright David Mamet checks out our scene, is inspired to make movies about con artists.

'97 ***"The Birthday Party Tour!"*** celebrates our tenth anniversary with 60 shows in 44 days in 18 towns across New England. Rob Mermin's book, *Circus Smirkus: A True Story of High Adventure and Low Comedy* is published with foreword by Marcel Marceau. Silent, but written with real words.

'98 ***"50's Rock 'n Roll Tour"*** rocks our new 750-seat Big Top from Italy! Troupers from USA, Russia, Mongolia, Israel and China. First exchange with the Wuqiao Acrobatic School. Smirkos win *People's Choice Award* at the Swedish International Circus Festival. One hundred children in the audience come in the ring each show to learn how to dance *"The Twist."* Smirkos perform with the Vermont Symphony Orchestra at First Night, forcing the conductor to conduct wearing a red clown nose. Tuba players bemused.

'99 ***"The Adventures of Robin Hood"*** romps through Martha's Vineyard and other New England villages. The Disney Channel films entire summer. Smirkus initiates annual visits to Paul Newman's Hole in the Wall Gang Camp. Legendary circus artist Alberto Zoppé and family bring their Percheron horses into the ring! Marcel Marceau gives smashing benefit performance in the big top alongside troupers. Smirko high-wire sky-walker wins place in Guinness Book of World Records. Hollywood producer Norman Lear brings comedian Dom DeLuise to catch the show. Does it ever get better than this?

'00 ***"Voyage of the Pirate Queen"*** storms the East Coast with troupers from 5 countries and 7 states. IndoKids from Indonesia join the tour. Smirkus dubbed "The United Nations of the Youth Circus World" at the International Children's Festival at Wolf Trap Park near Washington, D.C. Smirkus performs with *Sesame Street's* Bob McGrath. Disney Channel broadcasts "*Totally Circus,"* a 15-part Smirkus weekly TV series, shown around the world. Wearing a Smirkus T-shirt gets you recognized in airports everywhere... Smirkos in public places nervously anticipate getting pied.

'01 ***"Sci-Fi Smirkus: A Space Idiocy"*** blasts off with 72 shows in 7 weeks. First appearance by The Chicago Boyz and full collaboration with directors of Chicago's Midnight Circus. Arab and Israeli kids from Jerusalem perform together in the Smirkus ring. Chef Julia Child joins the Smirkus Honorary Board after eating at our pie car. Smirkus is at Wolf Trap Park on 9/11, as performing groups from several countries at the International Festival bond in the Smirkus tent.

'02 ***"Legends of the Wild West"*** rides into town with six-member bluegrass band, The Route 7 Ramblers. Square-dancing rocks the tent. First Nation Indian dancers and cowboy trick ropers from the Southwest bring the old West alive. Smirkus Advanced Campers create Road Show to tour senior centers and hospitals each year. Annie Oakley dances on the wire and shoots holes in the big top.

Highlights in the Limelight!

'03 ***"The Legion of Laughter: Superheroes of Smirkopolis"*** soars into action with young performers from Sweden's Cirkus and Variete. Smirkus School Residency programs expand, and Smirkus Camp adds Smirkling and Family sessions. Year-round staff grows to 10, seasonal staff to 100. The cows move to quieter pastures.

'04 ***"Smirkus: Through the Looking Glass"*** escorts audience down the rabbit hole with directors Jeff and Julie Jenkins. Students from Volunteers For Peace join us from Spain, France, England and Poland. Smirkus featured on *The Martha Stewart Show* as she goes off the air. (Was it us?) Smirkus professional alumni gather for a hot summer show on the stage at SeaWorld San Antonio. Dolphins next door catch every show.

'05 ***"Pinocchio"*** comes alive through collaboration with master puppeteers from The Sandglass Theater. Cirkestra, led by Peter Bufano, makes music for second season on the Smirkus bandstand. Miniature donkeys Jiminy and Figaro chase Gepetto around the ring and play with kids ringside. Tent crew competes with donkeys in back-lot braying contests. Crew wins, naturally.

'06 ***"Tropical Vacation"*** blends Hawaiian dancers and ukeleles with the debut of directors Troy Wunderle and Jesse Dryden—in grass skirts. Smirkus Camp welcomes kids from The Big Apple Circus after-school program in collaboration between "downtown and hometown."

'07 ***"The Zoot Suit Caper"*** welcomes international performers from Colombia, France and Mongolia. The swinging musical spy thriller (who "pied" the ringmaster?) has Troy Wunderle being pied in the face over 350 times on tour. It takes only two and a half bars of shaving soap to whip up 100 thick soapy pies. (Do not try this at home. Try it at a friend's house.)

'08 ***"Smirkusology: A Science Extravaganza"*** fills the ring with bubbles and magic experiments. EthioCircus and CirColombia form new bonds with Smirkus. Composer, musician and bandleader Tristan Moore joins the company. Founder Rob Mermin honored with Governor's Award for Excellence in the Arts. That doesn't keep the mud from stranding circus vehicles in the legendary Kennebunkport Mud Slide of '08 in Maine.

'09 ***"Smirkus Ever After: A Big Top Fairy Tale"*** produces fractured tales with 3 juggling pigs, flying witches, the tortoise and the hare, balancing bears, giants, Rapunzel, Hansel and Gretel and an assortment of other familiarly fantastical characters. Children go home dreaming Happily Ever Laughter.

'10 ***"Wilderness Wonders"*** collaborates with the National Park Ser-

vice to produce a show-full of four-season outdoor adventures in the ring, including a freezing snow blizzard, a ghostly campfire, a rainstorm, ice-skating clowns, Bigfoot—and a visit from a former U.S. President and First Lady, complete with Secret Service detail. Troy Wunderle initiates the First Smirkus Boss Clown Olympics: his antics get him appointed official Director of Clowning for all Ringling Bros. and Barnum & Bailey Circus productions. The world needs slapstick more than ever.

'11 ***"Front Page Follies"*** hits newsstands everywhere, making headlines with offbeat reports of raucous circus action disrupting daily life in towns throughout New England. But hold the presses! Once again the show is historically bogged down deep in mud at the bottom of Killington Mt., the trucks and caravans slip-sliding away to the next town. Clean white socks ordered for the tent crew.

'12 ***"Topsy-Turvy Time Travel"*** It's the 25th Anniversary Celebration Tour! Smirkus directors head to Cuba to teach and produce a show. Students from the National Circus School of Cuba, associated with Circuba, join Smirkus on the summer tour for the first U.S./Cuba youth circus cultural exchange. Vermont filmmaker Signe Taylor's feature documentary *Circus Dreams* airs on public television stations around the country. Journalist Rob Gurwitt and Smirkus founder Rob Mermin write the new book *Circus Smirkus: 25 Years of Running Home to the Circus.* That's the one in your hands right now, dear reader.

An Interview with Executive Director Ed LeClair

You arrived in 2003 and have been executive director since 2004. What do you see as the biggest changes to Smirkus since your arrival?

Paychecks. We get them on a fairly regular basis now. That wasn't a given in 2003.

Besides that, the whole world has changed. When Rob first started, "circus" was a disreputable word. Now Cirque du Soleil is a household name. Circus acts are integrated into the Academy Awards. Rock stars use "circus" as their tour theme. There are over 100 members in the American Youth Circus Organization. It's everywhere.

We see the results every day at Smirkus. Kids who audition now are more skilled and better trained. Our audiences are better educated about circus arts. Smirkus Camp is swamped with kids wanting to learn more about circus. Everywhere I look, the circus is experiencing a renaissance.

Does all that interest and available talent change how you run Circus Smirkus?

Sure. It's transformed our entire creative process. Rob focused on the Russian connection and all those world-class coaches because Smirkus needed to build the kids' skills. Once the kids became proficient, Jeff and Julie brought in the concept of a coordinated, professional production team to use lights, music and choreography to showcase the Smirkos' emerging talents.

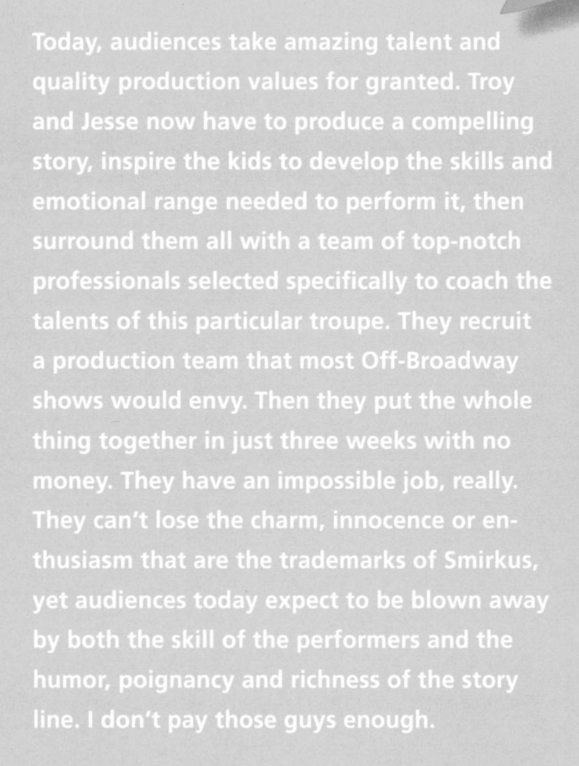

Today, audiences take amazing talent and quality production values for granted. Troy and Jesse now have to produce a compelling story, inspire the kids to develop the skills and emotional range needed to perform it, then surround them all with a team of top-notch professionals selected specifically to coach the talents of this particular troupe. They recruit a production team that most Off-Broadway shows would envy. Then they put the whole thing together in just three weeks with no money. They have an impossible job, really. They can't lose the charm, innocence or enthusiasm that are the trademarks of Smirkus, yet audiences today expect to be blown away by both the skill of the performers and the humor, poignancy and richness of the story line. I don't pay those guys enough.

It's the same story at Smirkus Camp. We've had so many talented kids applying we had to develop "Advanced Camp." The kids specialize in and choose between ensemble work, creating individual audition pieces or developing their performing chops on "Road Show," the camp's one-week tour. Each of those kids could perform before an audience and bring the house down. The trick is to build a program that simultaneously challenges them, feeds their love of circus and still lets them be kids.

Smirkus seems like it is doing well now, but things haven't always been so rosy. You had to close the doors in 2005. What happened to turn things around?

When we shut down in 2005, it proved that the world was changing and that we had to organize ourselves differently, create a new model. We had three main things that needed changing. First, we had to get more money in the door. People love Smirkus, so we had to make it easy for them to buy tickets, register for camp, contract for residencies and contribute to the cause. Second, the incredibly dedicated staff was burning out. We had to streamline their work. We put in budgets, annual calendars and planning systems so that staff could prepare instead of just reacting all the time. Finally we had to stay committed to balancing all these systems, practices and policies with the carefree, never-take-yourself-too-seriously, dreams-can-come-true culture that is our whole reason for being. Recently I signed a purchase order for green Irish derbies for the staff's St. Patrick's Day party. Seems like we're striking the balance pretty well.

You've set up a cultural exchange with Cuba. Are you still inviting international kids to Smirkus?

Yes, but it's not just about the talent. In the old days circuses presented exotic acts: sword swallowers from Borneo, pygmy jugglers from India, gauchos from the Pampas who could lasso a gnat. Acts like that sold tickets. But they also had an unexpected consequence. Long before people cared about "diversity," circuses created a place where people from vastly different cultures could work together and create something that pulled people to their feet in appreciation and wonder. This is too important to lose just because popular culture is embracing circus and skilled local kids are available. The words "traditional circus" are in our mission. That implies a responsibility to showcase what human beings really are capable of, with as wide a representation of people as we can.

Are other things about Smirkus "too important to lose"?

Absolutely. Everyone thinks my job is to make Smirkus financially sustainable, and partly it is. But the mantra I have for myself is, "Protect the whimsy." American culture has a habit of finding something charming and precious and turning it into a product or finding the most beautiful, inviting spot possible, paving it over and naming the mall after it.

Every kid wants to steal away to Narnia or Middle Earth or Never-Never-Land. They want to live where life is full of adventure and every day is a hero's journey. The real essence, the alchemy of Circus Smirkus, is that it allows kids to remain firmly planted in the enchanted, innocent, carefree world of childhood, but at the same time introduces them to the very real adult demands of self-discipline, cooperation and responsibility. And it's not a book, it's real. That is worth preserving.

What does the future look like?

Hmmm...you'll have to buy a ticket and see the show. No performer reveals how the act ends.

Every time I try to look forward, I keep reflecting back to the original vision: Circus Smirkus is a place where, with hard work and dedication, kids can make their dreams come true. A ring where those who jump in are accepted for what they contribute to the show, not their wealth or skin color or creed. I always say ***the function of circus is to astound and amaze,*** and in the Smirkus ring a wildly diverse group of people create a kaleidoscopic marvel that simultaneously defies gravity, passivity and the apathy of modern culture.

All I can tell you is that the future will be based on every kid's dream of running home to the circus. Rob Mermin and the caravan of characters that followed him launched a miracle under canvas. It is an incredible honor to be even a small part of it.

Curtain Call

I was once announced by a tongue-tied emcee as "the Flounder of Circus Smirkus." I thought it aptly described my improvisational approach to the company's misadventures over the years. I no longer have an active role in management, though I still put in my two cents as a creative advisor and return often to encourage kids to bend a few rules. In writing this book I have been in contact with several generations of far-flung troupers. It has reminded me how profoundly grateful I am to be a part of their lives. The bond among Smirkos is deep and lifelong; it is a family made strong through the shared experience of adventure. And each generation of troupers has left a unique stamp on the company. It truly is, and always has been, their circus. They are ambassadors of dreams.

I love watching little kids come up to the troupers for autographs after a show. They have awe on their faces and dreams in their eyes as they look up to performers who are only a few years older. I also look up to these troupers. Each has achieved moments in the ring that touch brilliance; it is achingly moving to witness. They have found something they love, worked hard and joyfully at it and put their whole hearts into it, which is rare these days. They move people not just with their breathtaking athletic skills, but the honesty of their presence, their playful individuality and the generosity of their youthful spirit. I see adults open-mouthed with wonder, sometimes blinking a tear away.

I have moved on-—teaching, directing, performing—but I cannot deny the pull of going out under canvas once more. The sawdust gets in your veins. The caravan lifestyle is a simpler way, and part of me is drawn to the idea of once again packing a bag with clown nose and baggy pants, sticking fifty dollars in my pocket, and heading off to Europe to find a circus. I mentioned this to a young performer and he looked at me quizzically, as if to say, "Does anyone do that anymore?" I smiled, shrugged and raised my hand, as if to respond...

—Why not?

See you down the road,

Rob Mermin

Dictionary, Smiktionary

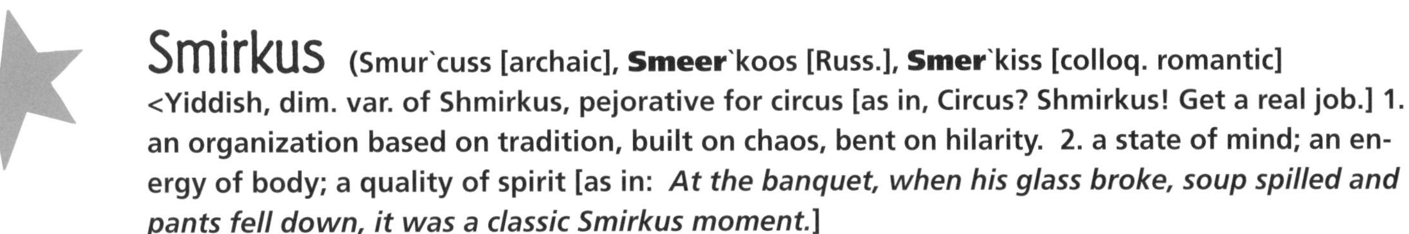

Smirkus (Smur`cuss [archaic], **Smeer**`koos [Russ.], **Smer**`kiss [colloq. romantic] <Yiddish, dim. var. of Shmirkus, pejorative for circus [as in, Circus? Shmirkus! Get a real job.] 1. an organization based on tradition, built on chaos, bent on hilarity. 2. a state of mind; an energy of body; a quality of spirit [as in: *At the banquet, when his glass broke, soup spilled and pants fell down, it was a classic Smirkus moment.*]

Smirko (**Smur**`ko), < n. anyone of any age who takes part in the high adventure and low comedy of a **Circus Smirkus** experience [as in: *A troupe of Smirkos performing under the Big Top will warm the smirkles of your heart.*]

Smirkling, <n. a baby Smirko. also adj. cute, talented, enthusiastic, independent. See also: smirkle, smirquant, smirkous, smirkable, smirkified [also smirkofied], besmirked, smirked [as in: *I Got Smirked!*]

Syn. there simply is no equivalent.

A Quarter Century Of Smirkus Troupers

Troupers Through the Years
Sonja Clawson, 1987
Pasquale DeMaio, 1987
Austin Hall, 1987
Alex Johnson, 1987
Danika Johnson, 1987
Pete Johnson, 1987
Ian Stearns, 1987
Aaron Stocek, 1987
David Weiner, 1987
Joss Williams, 1987
Nicholas Ponzio, 1987 - 1988
Sara Jesse, 1987 - 1988
Duane Barnett, 1987 - 1990
Lilias Ide, 1987 - 1990
Toby Ayer, 1987 - 1994
Jade Kindar-Martin, 1988 - 1994
Molly Saudek, 1988 - 1994
Molly Pelley, 1988 - 1995
Rachel Covey, 1988
Jesse Huffman, 1988
Sarah Sleeper, 1988
Mathew Colbert, 1988 - 1990
Emery Damon, 1988 - 1990
Nolan Haims, 1988, 1990
Alisa Leib, 1988 - 1990
Nate Cole, 1989 - 1990
Melissa Crandall, 1989 - 1990
Linden Ide, 1989 - 1990
Kate Podolec, 1989 - 1990
Katie Slavinski, 1989 - 1990
Sarah Dilley, 1989 - 1991
Porter Lontz-Underhill, 1989 - 1993
Addie MacDonald, 1989 - 1992
Casey Pickett, 1989 - 1992
Nathan Barnett, 1989 -1990
Libby Keith, 1991 - 1993
Ruslan Anokhin, 1990
Natalia Augustova, 1990
Irina Burdetskaya, 1990
Dasha Castellano, 1990
Jesse Hewitt, 1990
Ekaterina Ignatova, 1990
Mikhael Ivanov, 1990
Philip Kanishchev, 1990
Fransva Kotlyar, 1990
Nicholas Little, 1990
Nicholas Moran, 1990
Ludmilla Nikolaeva, 1990
Peter Saraoh, 1990
Ben Tolpin, 1990
Gregory Yudin, 1990
Adriana Agri, 1991
Ingride Bickhare, 1991
Alla Chernikova, 1991
Viktor Dodonov, 1991
Yuri Guseva, 1991
Maya Guseva, 1991
Andrei Ilin, 1991
Gennady Kantarovich, 1991
Tatiana Kutnevskaya, 1991
David McIntire, 1991
Tatiana Nepomniaschaya, 1991
Kuna Tavalin, 1991
Armand Zheivats, 1991
Doug Bair, 1991 - 1998
Chris Grabher, 1991 - 2000
Jamie Armantrout, 1992 - 1993
Maria Abesheva, 1992
Cris Clark, 1992
Heather Cox Tzall, 1992
Kourtney Groves, 1992
Staci Groves, 1992
Christi Higden, 1992
Adrienne Holst, 1992
Erin Leebolt, 1992
Jennie Olufson, 1992
Maxim Pantaleeke, 1992
Alexei Prikhodko, 1992
Nadegga Solosena, 1992
Leonid Viero, 1992
Ivan Youdin, 1992
Erin Cox Keyser, 1992 - 1993
Scott Higden, 1992 - 1993
Kate Hayes, 1992 - 1997
Andrew Adams,1992 - 1998
Jenni Martinez, 1992
Treena Agecoutay, 1993
Lisa Bobbish, 1993
Rachel Bobbish, 1993
Elena Kudreachova, 1993
Vladimir Malashikhin, 1993
John Pashe, 1993
Murray Pashe, 1993
Sam Pashe, 1993
Eugena Solovena, 1993
Elena Tukene, 1993
Nathan Weedward, 1993
Tyrone Young Bear, 1993
Lisa Taylor-Parisi, 1993 - 1998
Richard Saudek, 1993 - 1997
Sam Johnson, 1993 - 1998
Vanessa Lind, 1993 - 1998
Anastassia Bagrova, 1994
Chris Bongiorno, 1994
Artem Hemarko, 1994
Eugene Shmarlouski, 1994
Anastassia Tarassova, 1994
Vera Tarassova, 1994
Viktor Teslenko, 1994
Sogna Tsogthbaatar, 1994
Mike Warshaw, 1994
Dan Good, 1994 - 1996
David Sbordoni, 1994 - 1996
Beth Carpenter, 1994 - 1997
Chris Molinski, 1994 - 1997
Mike Plotz, 1994 - 1999
Tamir Bayarsaihan, 1994 - 2001, 2003
Adam Kuchler, 1995
Anton Milaev, 1995
Zoltan Zoboky, 1995 - 1996
Nick Curran, 1995 - 1998
Juliana Frick, 1995 - 2000
Tristan Cunningham, 1995 - 2002
Rachel Schiffer, 1995 - 2004
Phil Leef, 1996
Max Pantaleenko, 1996
Javier "Gordo" Valentin, 1996
Russell Towl, 1996 - 1997
Callie Fentress, 1996 - 1999
Ben Reynolds, 1996 - 2000
Vincent Churchill, 1996 - 2001
Francey Grund, 1996 - 2002
Amanda Crockett, 1997 - 1998
Meredith Maglio, 1997 - 1998
Leo Sblendorio, 1997 - 1998
Sarah Geismer, 1997 - 1999
Raber Umphenour, 1997 - 1999
Patrick Mannion, 1997 - 2004
Qiuyu Chen, 1998
Stryder Crown, 1998
DJ Delaney Gillilan, 1998
Guo Zhanghui, 1998
Li Bao, 1998
Stefy Rompas, 1998
Larisa Sitorus, 1998
Sunyoto, 1998
Yang Xiaomei, 1998
Dylan Fuller, 1998 - 1999
Hyla Gayer, 1998 - 1999
Olivia Oller, 1998 - 1999, 2001 - 2004
Julia Kaminsky, 1998 - 2000

Steve Schubart, 1998 - 2000
John Stokvis, 1998 - 2002
Case Conover, 1999
Nerida Dawkin, 1999
Bolorerderne Ulziisaikhan, 1999
Khulan Urnult, 1999
Joe Waudby, 1999
Dasha Sergatcheva-Bochenko, 1999 - 2000
Sian Flatt, 1999 - 2000, 2002
Ariele Ebacher, 1999 - 2001
Willow Yonika, 1999 - 2001
Dan Brown, 1999 - 2002
Sam Brown, 1999 - 2002
Ian Caldwell, 1999 - 2002
Ryan Combs, 1999 - 2002
Kaleen McKeeman, 1999 - 2002
David Graham, 1999 - 2003
Thora Graham, 1999 - 2003
Kerren McKeeman, 1999 - 2003
Sajana Blank, 1999 - 2004
Alex Friedlander-Moore, 1999 - 2005
Jacob Skeffington, 1999, 2001 - 2002
Tobin Renwick, 1999 - 2003
Enkhtsataral Enkhjargal, 2000
Saditgel Ganbaatar, 2000
Josh Shack, 2000 - 2003
Bret Pfister, 2000 - 2004
Abby Suskin, 2000 - 2005
Liz Gibson, 2001
Alex Karoff-Hunger, 2001
Ella Thorne-Thomsen, 2001
Tim Weeks, 2001
Omar Dudley, 2001 - 2002
Nicky Pearson, 2001 - 2002
John Stork, 2001 - 2003
Michou Tchana Hyman, 2001 - 2003
Isabel Patrowicz, 2001 - 2006
Jody Bear, 2002
Micah Burke, 2002

Derek Cheney, 2002
Devin Davenport, 2002
Deanna Favel, 2002
Trent Gamble, 2002
Sean "Spike"McGuire, 2002
Nick McReynolds, 2002
Jaime Venmar, 2002 - 2003
Zoey Phillips, 2002 - 2004
Yolante Birkhane, 2003
Henry Glick, 2003
Lael Skeffington, 2003
Mike Richter, 2003 - 2004
Jake Verner, 2003 - 2004
Elin Andersson, 2003 - 2005
Jacob Bloom, 2003 - 2006
Eric Brown, 2003 - 2006
Lydia Brosnahan, 2003 - 2006, 2008
Kia Melinda Eastman, 2003 - 2008
Jen Agans, 2004
Woodrow Travers, 2004
Emmanuel Turner, 2004
Mason Ames, 2004 - 2005
Erica Bates, 2004 - 2005
Tristan Nielsen, 2004 - 2005
Jacob Sherry, 2004 - 2005
Patrick Tobin, 2004 - 2005
Hazel Briner, 2004 - 2007
Sam Galison, 2004 - 2007
Jacob Stein-Sharpe, 2004 - 2007
Book Kennison, 2004 - 2008
Ariana Ferber-Carter, 2004 - 2009
Henry Cesari, 2005
Marston Leff, 2005
Hanna Lilly Postman, 2005
Spencer Novich, 2005 - 2006
Nate Stein-Sharpe, 2005 - 2007
Thea Ulrich, 2005 - 2006
Chelsea Brooklyn, 2005 - 2006, 2008
Katie Sickles, 2005 - 2007
Greylin Nielsen, 2005 - 2008, 2010

Ben Bond, 2005 - 2009
Dylan Friedman, 2006
Joseph Montano, 2006
Raphael Benjamin, 2006 - 2007
Cat Claus, 2006 - 2007
Maddy Hall, 2006 - 2007
Joy Powers, 2006 - 2007
Eric Allen, 2006 - 2008
Thula Martin, 2006 - 2008
Lindsay Culbert-Olds, 2006 - 2009
Jacob Tischler, 2006 - 2009
Daniel Sullivan, 2006 - 2010
Taylor Wright-Sanson, 2006 - 2010
Angel Casierra, 2007
Sylphie Currin, 2007
Odiargal Enerel, 2007
Choogjoo Gerelchimeg, 2007
Janoah Bailin, 2007 - 2008
Isabelle Schuster, 2007 - 2008
Josh Aviner, 2007 - 2009
Aerial Emery, 2007 - 2009
Sebastian Kann, 2007 - 2009
Arne Bystrom, 2008
Tersit Asefa Dersu, 2008
Anastasia Dickenson, 2008
Eyerusalum Moges Getachew, 2008
Francisco Javier Hartado, 2008
Ayal Prouser, 2008
Leidy Tatiana Zainiga Vidal, 2008
Shea Vaccaro, 2008 - 2009
Zora Blade, 2008 - 2010
Jared Mongeau, 2008 - 2010
Jamie Nanni, 2008 - 2010
Frances Tiffin, 2008 - 2010
Owen Winship, 2008 - 2011
Emma Bradford, 2009
Fiona Lowry, 2009
Lillian Maltz, 2009
Emmanuel Ribereau, 2009
Anna Conway, 2009 - 2010

Aaron DeWitt, 2009 - 2010
Shane Miclon, 2009 - 2010
Leah Samelson, 2009 - 2010
Al Mireault, 2009 - 2011
Collin Miclon, 2010 - 2011
Julia Greenberg, 2010 - 2011
Zoe Ruth Silberblatt, 2010 - 2011
John Stubbs, 2010 - 2011
Aaron Berman, 2010 - 2012
Sellam "Whistle" Cottle El Ouahabi, 2010, 2012
Maia Gawor-Sloane, 2010 - 2012
Magnus Giaever, 2010 - 2012
Alyson Mattei, 2010 - 2012
Noah Nielsen, 2010 - 2012
Jessica Roginsky, 2010 - 2012
Olivia Saunders, 2010 - 2012
Ezra Weill, 2010 - 2012
Nick Zelle, 2010 - 2012
Chase Culp, 2011 - 2012
Una Bennett, 2011 - 2012
Sam Ferlo, 2011 - 2012
Emily Gare, 2011 - 2012
Sam Gurwitt, 2011 - 2012
Sonya Gurwitt, 2011 - 2012
Bekk McGowan, 2011 - 2012
Willem McGowan, 2011 - 2012
Anna Partridge, 2011 - 2012
Morgan Pinney, 2011 - 2012
Emma Rogers, 2011 - 2012
Brin Schoellkopf, 2011 - 2012
Sarah Tiffin, 2011 - 2012
Emily Wunderle, 2011 - 2012
Isa Ansari, 2012
Marieke Dailey, 2012
Liam Gundlach, 2012
Remi Sanchez, 2012
Keenan Wright-Sanson, 2012
Ricardo Guevara Balart, 2012
Yazmil Betancourt Padron, 2012

Acknowledgements

A Final Word of Thanks...

Ed LeClair and the Circus Smirkus board of directors not only saw the promise in this project, they gave it the financial backing that ushered it into print.

An incredible number of people lent us their time, memories and insights, entertaining us with their stories and informing every nook and cranny of this book. Some of them got quoted directly, many did not, but all of them helped us understand Smirkus better. They include: Aaron Berman, Abby Suskin, Alla Youdina, Ariele Ebacher, Barb Baird, Beth LeCoeurs, Betsy van Gemeren, Bill Forchion, Bret Pfister, Brita Larson, Caleb Elder, Casey Pickett, CharAnn Brown, Chimgee Haltarhuu, Chris Butler, Chris Combs, Chris Grabher, Cris Clark, Dan Brown, Dick Saudek, Donny Osman, Elena Esteban, Elsie Smith, Francey Grund, Ian Caldwell, Rabbi Ira Schiffer, Jack Stokvis, Jade Kindar-Martin, Jay Craven, Jeff Jenkins, Father Jerry Hogan, Jesse Dryden, Jessica Labun, Jim and Debby Sharpe, John Stork, Josh Shack, Judy Gaeth, Julie Jenkins, Kaleen McKeeman, Katie Schroeder, Kerren McKeeman, Lilias Ide, Lucie Patrowicz, Maia Gawor-Sloane, Marcel Marceau, Marialisa Calta, Mary Blouin Auffert, Mason Ames, Megan Rose, Molly Saudek, Nat Brown, Nick Zelle, Nolan Haims, Ozzie Henchel, Patrick Mannion, Peter Bufano, Porter Lontz-Underhill, Rachel Schiffer, Sajana Blank, Sam Brown, Sam Gurwitt, Sam Johnson, Sam Pashe, Sara Wunderle, Scott Higdon, Serenity Smith Forchion, Sonya Gurwitt, Stewart Lippe, Tamir Bayarsaihan, Ted Lawrence, Toby Ayer, Tosca Zoppé, Tristan Cunningham, Tristan Moore, Troy Wunderle and Willow Yonika. We are indebted to all of you and deeply aware that in the limited space we had, we couldn't possibly do justice to your generous spirits.

We gained immeasurably from the help of Ben Winship and Katherine Dickson, who stepped in to do interviews when we were overwhelmed. Josh Browne cheerfully helped us negotiate the minutiae of self-publishing and gave us a running start with booksellers.

We owe a special debt to three people. Wendy Ruopp was our copy editor, a term that doesn't do justice to her deft, incisive and eagle-eyed talents. Serena Fox, our graphic designer, poured more of her time, immense skill and deep well of creativity into this project than we had any right to ask; she pondered and fretted over every page, and if you enjoyed the process of looking through them, you have her to thank. And Karen Harris, Rob G.'s wife, has lived with this book as long as we have; whether she likes it or not, her good humor, boundless patience and warm-hearted insights make her our partner in crime.

Then there are all the people who have helped make Smirkus what it is. Marialisa Calta, Elena Esteban, Judy Gaeth, Sara Wunderle, Danielle Kehlmann, Angela Bittner, Megan Rose and Vanessa Gengler of Smirkus World Headquarters work behind the scenes year-round to keep Smirkus visible and functional. And we'd be remiss if we didn't mention the tent bosses who have kept the show on the road over 25 years: Dave Lucas, Paul Ide, Chris Butler, Erik Jaeger, Giovanni Zoppé, Jay Walther, Ivan Hennessey, Logan Upson, Nat Brown. Gordon and Pat Richardson, our neighbors, have graciously allowed Smirkus to pitch its tent on their land for all this time.

Our final thanks go to the people who aren't named: the ones who founded the many circus schools around the country that have trained young talent showcased in the Smirkus ring; the thousands of parents over the years who have been so brave and nutty as to allow their kids the chance to explore their dreams as part of Smirkus; the members of the staff and crew who shared the love, grit and resolve it takes to bring delight into the ring; and above all the schoolkids, campers and troupers who stepped out of everyday life, reached beyond what they ever dreamed possible and left a bit of themselves in the hearts of everyone who saw them.

Rob & Rob
June 2012
robmermin.com
robgurwitt.com
smirkus.org

Smirkus Around the World

The number of states troupers come from:

26

The number of Native American Tribes (Assiniboine, Dakota, Sioux, Cree, Yakima, Oglala, Hunkpapa, Navaho, Lakota, Santee) under our Big Top:

10

Countries represented in our ring over the years:

32

Canada
China
Colombia
Cuba
Denmark
Ethiopia
France
Georgia
Germany
Hungary
Indonesia
Israel
Italy
Japan
Kazakhstan
Korea
Latvia
Mexico
Moldova
Mongolia
Morocco
Netherlands
New Zealand
Palestinian Authority
Poland
Russia
Spain
Sweden
Switzerland
Thailand
Ukraine
United Kingdom

Photo Credits

Frank Molinski
Bill Thompson
Gigi Kaeser
Glenn Russell
Mimi Leveque
Henry Olds
Robert Sanson
Harry Powers
Kate Russell

Additional photo contributions:

Dana Greenblatt
Morton Langkilde
Nicole Bengevino (The New York Times/Redux)
Karine Mauffrey
Steve Krasner
Steve Liss
Barry Hayes
Jym Wilson
Rose McNulty
Eric Workman
Denise Johnson
Toby Talbot

Rob Mermin, the founder of Circus Smirkus, ran off to Europe to begin a 40-year career in circus, theater and TV. He currently lives in Montpelier, Vermont.

Rob Gurwitt is a freelance writer who lives in Norwich, Vermont. He got to know Circus Smirkus on a magazine assignment in 1999, and he and his family have been entranced by circuses ever since.

Poster Design credits:

Keith Chamberlin
Sarah-Lee Terrat
Rob Mermin
Jana Zeller
Meryl Lebowitz
Troy Wunderle
Elena Esteban

We would like to thank the many talented photographers whose photos in our archives caught our eye but whose names eluded us. We sincerely apologize for any mistakes we have made in compiling photos for the book.

VERMONT'S OWN HOME-GROWN COUNTRY CIRCUS
TIGHTROPE
TRAPEZE
CLOWNS
JUGGLERS
CIRCUS SMIRKUS
FIRE-EATERS
ACROBATS
1989 TOUR
PLACE:
DATE:
TIME:
TICKET INFO:
SPONSORED BY:

CIRCUS
ЦИРК
MOSCOW CIRCUS
MEETS
CIRCUS SMIRKUS
Direct from the famous Moscow Circus School
Vermont's own home-grown country circus
1990
USA • USSR TOUR
co-produced by: Project Harmony

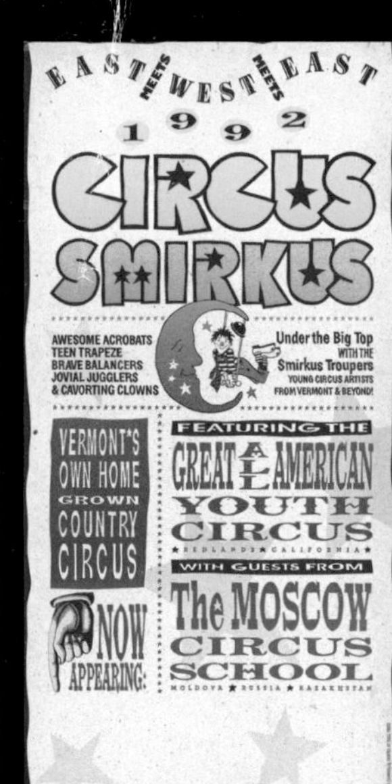

EAST MEETS WEST MEETS EAST
1992
CIRCUS SMIRKUS
AWESOME ACROBATS
TEEN TRAPEZE
BRAVE BALANCERS
JOVIAL JUGGLERS
& CAVORTING CLOWNS
Under the Big Top
WITH THE Smirkus Troupers
YOUNG CIRCUS ARTISTS FROM VERMONT & BEYOND!
VERMONT'S OWN HOME GROWN COUNTRY CIRCUS
NOW APPEARING:
FEATURING THE
GREAT ALL AMERICAN YOUTH CIRCUS
WITH GUESTS FROM
The MOSCOW CIRCUS SCHOOL

1 9 9 3
VERMONT'S HOME-GROWN COUNTRY CIRCUS
The PRINCESS WHO WOULDN'T LAUGH
THE MOSCOW YOUTH CIRCUS
INDIAN DANCERS
CIRCUS SMIRKUS
TIME
DATE
PLACE
TICKET INFO

CIRCUS SMIRKUS
PRESENTS
HOUDINI LIVES!
AND FOR THE POPULAR ENJOYMENT OF THE MASSES A FIRST CLASS
SIDE SHOW!
PRESTI-DIGITATION!
LEVITATION!
FIRE EATING!
AND MORE!
VERMONT'S HOME GROWN COUNTRY CIRCUS
TIME
DATE
PLACE
TICKET INFO

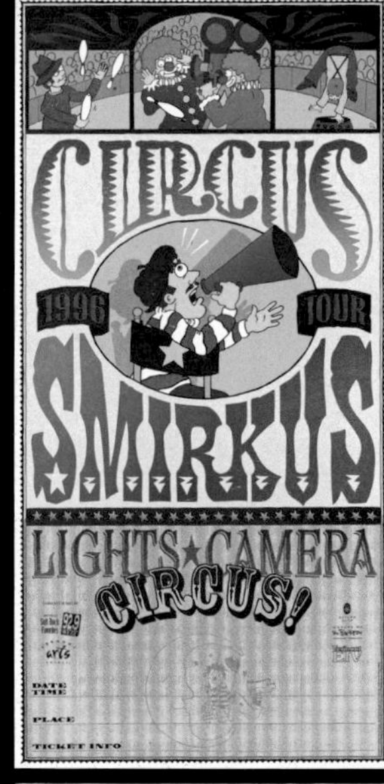

CIRCUS
1996
TOUR
SMIRKUS
LIGHTS★CAMERA
CIRCUS!
DATE
TIME
PLACE
TICKET INFO

CIRCUS SMIRKUS
1997
BIRTHDAY PARTY TOUR!
10
ANNIVERSARY!
DATE
TIME
PLACE
TICKET INFO

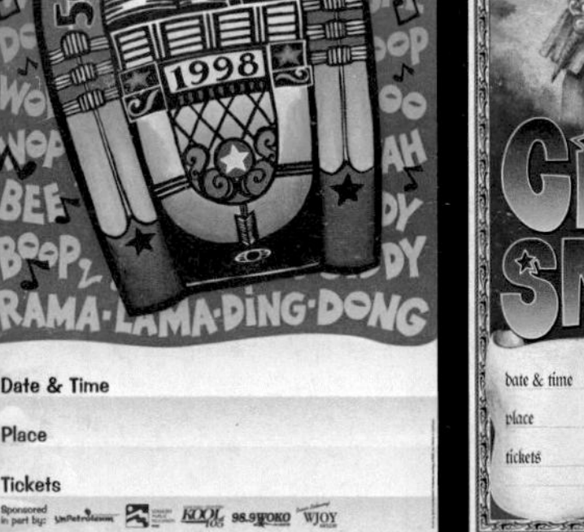

CIRCUS SMIRKUS
50's ROCK & ROLL TOUR
1998
RAMA-LAMA-DING-DONG
Date & Time
Place
Tickets

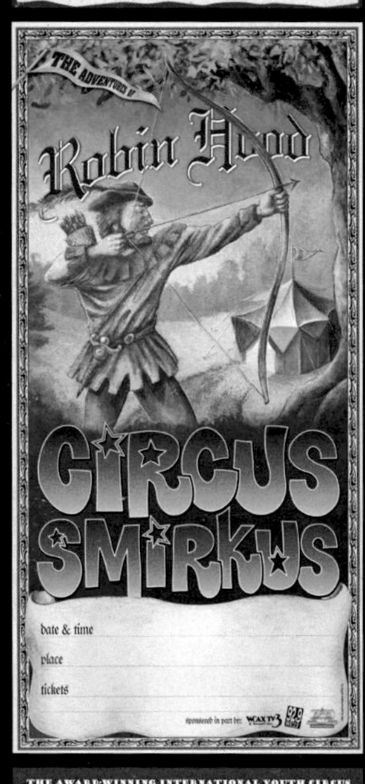

THE ADVENTURES OF
Robin Hood
CIRCUS SMIRKUS
date & time
place
tickets

CIRCUS SMIRKUS
The Voyage of the Pirate Queen
THE 2000 TOUR
Date & Time
Place
Tickets
Presented by

CIRCUS SMIRKUS
To Boldly Go Where No Clown Has Gone Before...
SciFi Tour 2001
Thurs – Sat., Aug. 16 – 18
7 PM Thurs – 10:30 & 7 PM Fri – 11 AM Sat
Montpelier High School
$12 / $10 in advance: tickets at Price Chopper, City Kids, JC Penny, Woodbury Mtn. Toys, or call:
The Circus Barn, 802-533-7443

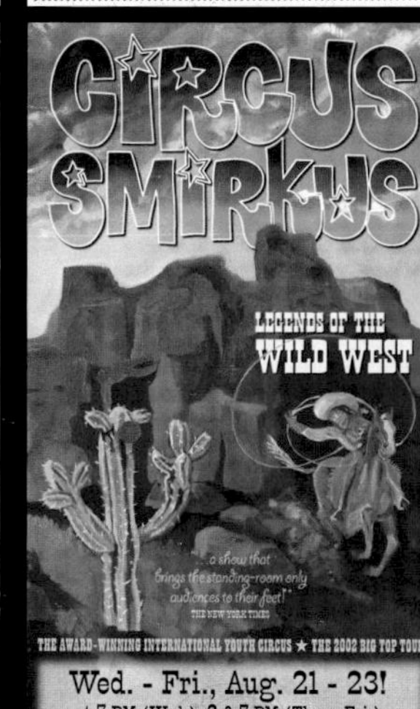

CIRCUS SMIRKUS
LEGENDS OF THE WILD WEST
THE AWARD-WINNING INTERNATIONAL YOUTH CIRCUS ★ THE 2002 BIG TOP TOUR
Wed. - Fri., Aug. 21 - 23!
at 7 PM (Wed.); 2 & 7 PM (Thu. - Fri.)
At Montpelier High School
Advance Tickets: $10 ★ At the Show: $12
Presented by the Circus Barn
www.smirkus.org

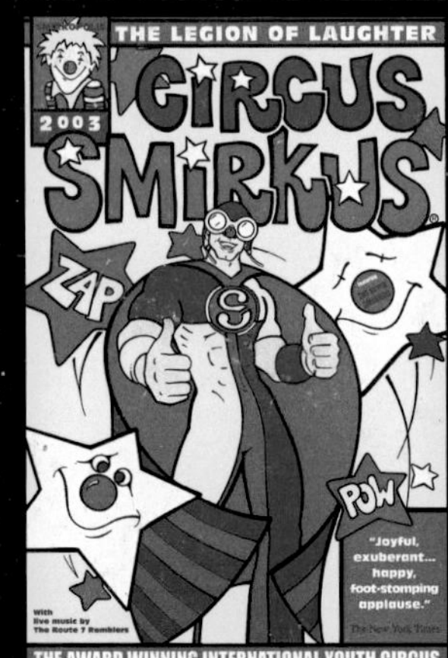

THE LEGION OF LAUGHTER
2003
CIRCUS SMIRKUS
ZAP
POW
"Joyful, exuberant... happy, foot-stomping applause."
THE AWARD WINNING INTERNATIONAL YOUTH CIRCUS
July 15 & 16 ★ 2 & 7 PM
Historic Fort Adams, Newport, RI
$12 Kids & Srs., $15 Adults & Superheros, $75 Arch Villians
Advanced tickets: Fort Adams Visitor Center, or call 800-532-7443
Presented by Circus Smirkus, with thanks to the Fort Adams Trust
WWW.SMIRKUS.ORG

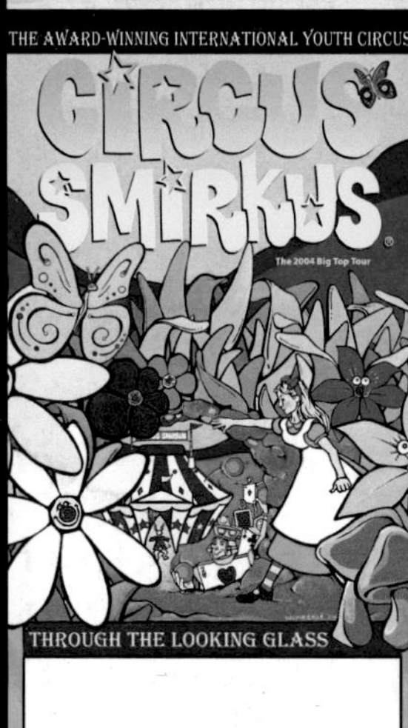

THE AWARD-WINNING INTERNATIONAL YOUTH CIRCUS
CIRCUS SMIRKUS
The 2004 Big Top Tour
THROUGH THE LOOKING GLASS
www.smirkus.org

THE AWARD-WINNING INTERNATIONAL YOUTH CIRCUS
CIRCUS SMIRKUS
THE 2005 TOUR
PINOCCHIO
WWW.SMIRKUS.ORG

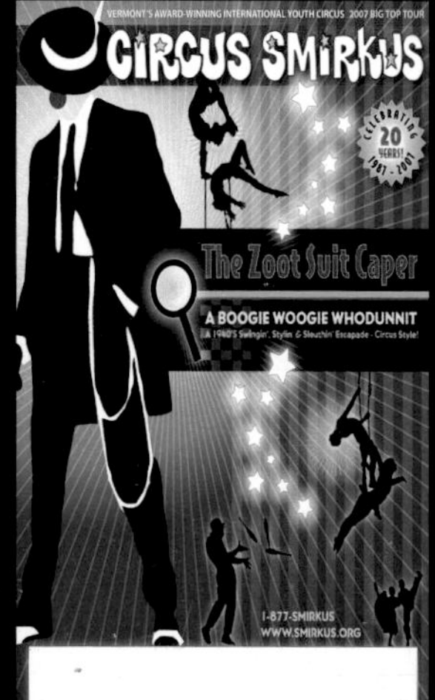

VERMONT'S AWARD-WINNING INTERNATIONAL YOUTH CIRCUS 2007 BIG TOP TOUR
CIRCUS SMIRKUS
CELEBRATING 20 YEARS
The Zoot Suit Caper
A BOOGIE WOOGIE WHODUNNIT
1-877-SMIRKUS
WWW.SMIRKUS.ORG

VERMONT'S AWARD-WINNING INTERNATIONAL YOUTH CIRCUS 2009 BIG TOP TOUR
CIRCUS SMIRKUS
Smirkus Ever After
A Big Top Fairytale
1-877-SMIRKUS
(1-877-764-7587)
WWW.SMIRKUS.ORG

VERMONT'S AWARD-WINNING INTERNATIONAL YOUTH CIRCUS 2011 BIG TOP TOUR
CIRCUS SMIRKUS
FRONTPAGE FOLLIES
Big Top Big News!
Clowns Around Town
Popcorn Promotes Promise
TICKETS
1-877-SMIRKUS
(1-877-764-7587)
SMIRKUS.ORG